ANIMACY IN RUSSIAN

UCLA Slavic Studies
Volume 6

ANIMACY IN RUSSIAN
A NEW INTERPRETATION

by

Emily Klenin

Slavica Publishers, Inc.
Columbus, Ohio

Slavica publishes a wide variety of books and journals dealing with the peoples, languages, literatures, history, folklore, and culture of the peoples of Eastern Europe and the USSR. For a complete catalog with prices and ordering information, please write to:

Slavica Publishers, Inc.
P.O. Box 14388
Columbus, Ohio 43214
USA

ISBN: 0-89357-115-6.

Text set by Kathleen McDermott at the East European Composition Center, supported by the Department of Slavic Languages and Literatures and the Center for Russian and East European Studies at UCLA.

Printed in the United States of America.

CONTENTS

ACKNOWLEDGMENTS

Most of the research on which this book is based was done at the National Humanities Center, where I was a Fellow in 1979–1980. I am especially grateful to W. A. Tuttle, Librarian of the Humanities Center, for extraordinary help in obtaining photocopies and other materials through interlibrary loan. Work on the Primary Chronicle was greatly facilitated by a concordance of it that I compiled, thanks to support from the American Philosophical Society, the Harvard Graduate Society, and the Harvard Ukrainian Research Institute. I am also grateful for the support of the UCLA Center for Russian and East European Studies (Bariša Krekić, Director), for a publication subsidy provided from the James Duke Endowment Fund. I also wish to thank the Department of Slavic Languages and Literatures, in particular the UCLA Slavic Studies Editorial Committee (Henrik Birnbaum, Thomas Eekman, Alan Timberlake). Earlier versions of the book were read in whole or in part by Horace Lunt, Susumu Kuno, Alan Timberlake, and Dean Worth, all of whom offered helpful suggestions. I am particularly grateful to Horace Lunt and Dean Worth for valuable discussion and substantive comments at several stages of the project.

Chapter One.   Introduction.

1. The Genitive-Accusative in Modern Russian.

In Modern Russian, there are two basic kinds of genitive-accusative case syncretism, and all Russian declension classes have one kind or the other.

The first type of syncretism is conditioned by, among other things, referential animacy. For example, the nouns *stol* 'table' and *kot* '(tom)cat' are masculine and belong to the same declension class, but their accusatives are, respectively, *stol* (like the nominative) and *kota* (like the genitive). In this declension class, referentially inanimate nouns have nominative-accusative syncretism, and all masculine animates have genitive-accusative syncretism.[1] However, nonmasculine (neuter) nouns, as well as all the nouns in other declension classes, restrict the genitive-accusative to the plural, where, as in the singular of nouns like *stol*, inanimate nouns have nominative-accusative syncretism. A few masculine nouns that are referentially inanimate, for example the dance called the *trepak*, nevertheless require the genitive-accusative in the singular. Nouns whose reference can be either animate or inanimate, for example *lico* 'face, persona, person', usually have genitive-accusative or nominative-accusative syncretism accordingly; however, some nouns whose inanimate reference is to cards or game pieces have the genitive-accusative regardless. Examples of this are *tuz*, which means not only 'ace' (its basic meaning) but also 'bigwig', and *slon*, which means both 'elephant' and 'bishop (in chess)'. Some inanimates permit limited variation between nominative- and genitive-accusative forms (see Ickovič 1980).

The other main type of genitive-accusative syncretism is restricted only by declension class, without regard to animacy. This kind of genitive-accusative is found in the declension of the anaphoric pronoun (for all genders and both numbers) and the reflexive pronoun *sebja* '(one)self'. Personal pronouns and the indefinite interrogative and relative pronoun *kto* 'who, what' fit in both categories at once, since their referents are always animate. Adjectives are syncretic if their heads are either syncretic (e.g. *tuz*) or referentially animate and masculine (e.g. *djadja* 'uncle', with nonsyncretic accusative singular *djadju*) or both (e.g. *kot*). The relative pronoun *kotoryj* 'who, which, that', with an adjectival declension pattern, is adjectival also with respect to the genitive-accusative, as are pronouns that can function syntactically as modifiers — e.g., the demonstratives *ètot* and *tot*, the emphatic *sam* '(one)self' and the quantifier *ves'* 'all'.[2] (See Chapter Six for more detail.) Below, the genitive-accusative will be treated in two main groups, noun and pronoun syncretism, but adjectives and the pronouns sensitive to animacy will be treated together with the nouns. The term "pronominal genitive-accusative" will thus be used to apply to the genitive-accusative in just those paradigms where it has been generalized.

The following chapters discuss both types of genitive-accusative syncretism, and examine their interrelations in some detail. Although the correlation of the Russian genitive-accusative with referential animacy is, of course, of great importance, the focus of our discussion will be the relation of the genitive-accusative, especially the animate-marking genitive-accusative, to other inflexional categories, in particular case (Chapter Five) and gender (Chapter Six).

The genitive-accusative has been written about extensively; instead of surveying the enormous body of literature on the subject, I intend only to examine certain problems that I have found interesting and that seem to me to have at least partial solutions.

2. *Some Problems in the Study of the Genitive-Accusative.*

Both genitive-accusative syncretism and its correlation with referential properties originated in prehistoric Common Slavic. This, of course, makes the actual innovation of the animate (at first probably mainly personal) genitive-accusative historically inaccessible, but, at the same time, it means that the Russian development can be compared with similar ones in the other Slavic languages, where virtually every logically possible development of the innovation is represented. On the whole, the important stages in the history of the genitive-accusative are well attested, and its correlation with referential properties has always been, as it is now, rather simple and intuitively easy to understand. The genitive-accusative thus is a readily accessible object of study, and has been approached from a number of different viewpoints, with varied theoretical purposes.

Durnovo's 1924 work on gender provides the basis for all later analyses of Russian animacy as a subgender (see Durnovo 1924, Jakobson 1959/1971 and 1960/1971, and Zaliznjak 1964, 1967), although Hjelmslev's 1956 study, approaching animacy first from the viewpoint of its semantics, treats animacy as superordinate to the sex-referential semantics of the Indoeuropean gender system inherited by Common Slavic. In her typology of Slavic gender, Karpinskaja (1966) to some extent reconciles these different approaches; Stankiewicz (1968b), on the other hand, extends the specifically Jakobsonian analysis to all of Slavic, and animacy is presented as an important, but subordinate, element in the gender system.

In addition, Russian animacy has been discussed as, historically, a syntactic or quasisyntactic phenomenon by, for example, Nekrasov (1905), Thomson

(1908, 1909, 1913), Šaxmatov (1910–1911/1957/1976), Sommer (1916), and Comrie (1976), all of whom have been concerned with the historic relation between genitive-accusative syncretism and syntactic genitive case marking. This was also one of the main concerns of Meillet's classic (1897) work on the Old Church Slavonic genitive-accusative, and it has been touched on in studies of other problems in Old Russian grammar (e.g. Timberlake 1974). Moreover, since the rise of the genitive-accusative is often taken (in my opinion, not entirely correctly) to involve the diachronic substitution of genitive-case forms for accusative ones, the relation of the genitive-accusative to syntactic genitive case usage of all types (the partitive genitive, the genitive of negation, the genitive object with verbs of perception, and some other lexically controlled genitives) has been discussed in most work on the origins of the genitive-accusative in Slavic (see e.g. Berneker 1904, Kuryłowicz 1962, and works by Meillet, Nekrasov, Thomson, and Sommer cited above).

It can be seen even from this cursory survey (and a detailed examination would show yet more clearly) that there is some tendency for the genitive-accusative to be treated in the general context of the Russian gender system in synchronic analyses, and in the context of case marking when it is studied diachronically. (Left out of account here are numerous studies, such as Kedajtene's, that provide rich documentation of the progress of the genitive-accusative in Old Russian writing, but that do not address broader issues.) Much rarer are analyses such as Nekrasov 1905 and van Schooneveld 1977, according to whom the genitive-accusative is and always has been a genitive case form. Although it is clear from Meillet 1897 that the genitive-accusative is unlikely to be usefully analyzed as a genitive case form, nevertheless, van Schooneveld's and Nekrasov's analyses are consistent in a way that few others are, and they sharply point up the usual disconnection between synchronic and diachronic studies of the Russian genitive-accusative. This discontinuity does not reflect an actual change in the genitive-accusative's grammatical status, but derives mainly from unexamined analytical assumptions. The historical uniformity of the genitive-accusative will be one of the most important theses of the analysis presented below.

We will discuss both historical and synchronic aspects of the Russian genitive-accusative, although no attempt has been made to offer either a full history or an exhaustive synchronic analysis. More pages are devoted to diachrony than to synchrony, for several reasons. One reason, purely practical, is that there is more left to say about the history than about the current status of the genitive-accusative — and this in spite of so much having already been written. Already existing synchronic analyses, such as Karpinskaja's and Stankiewicz's, offer excellent comprehensive coverage of their subject, whereas the historical studies have generally been either too sweeping to permit much examination of detail or too detailed to permit drawing many general conclusions. Works by Kedajtene, Dietze, and many others have presented exhaustive analyses of individual texts or texts from a single, short stage in the implementation of the genitive-accusative, or they have tended to study the genitive-accusative only as an expression of animacy in nouns, thus ignoring the history of the genitive-accusative in pronouns. On the other hand, the now classic works by Thomson and, to a lesser extent, Šaxmatov, although they inspired much of the work that came after them, nevertheless have been partly superseded by it. It is thus now possible to take a second look at some of the generalizations that Thomson, especially, offered, in the light of the several intervening generations of detailed textual studies.

Another reason for writing at such relative length about the history of the genitive-accusative (and, in particular about the history of the genitive-accusative in pronouns, where it is not directly correlated with animacy) is that a fairly detailed diachronic analysis will facilitate our reaching a better understanding of the genitive-accusative's modern status. The importance of connecting the genitive-accusative's history and synchrony has already been suggested, and we have noted that there is some tendency to lose sight of this relation. At the same time, however, there is one synchronic/diachronic connection that is so well established that it has become virtually a part of our intuitive understanding — and mistakenly so, I believe. Because of the extraordinary prestige of the theory in question, its refutation will occupy us at length. We can start here, by explaining what it is.

2.1. Functional Syntax Adumbrated: A. I. Thomson and the Classical Theory of the Rise of the Genitive-Accusative.

In Modern Russian, the expression of animacy and the status of the genitive-accusative are nearly entirely stable (although see Ickovič 1980 and Corbett 1980a). They are inaccessible to exploitation for stylistic purposes and only rarely exhibit variation from one speaker to another. Because the informational value of the modern genitive-accusative is so low, it is often thought to represent only the impoverished heir to an earlier situation, in which genitive-accusative syncretism had a more obvious function, namely to mark nominative-syncretic direct objects as genitive-case objects, so that they could not be mistaken for (nominative) subjects. Old Russian made extensive use of genitive-case verbal objects, and it has been suggested that the genitive-accusative originated as one more genitive object, similar to the genitive partitive objects or to objects of negated verbs or of verbs such as *ždat'* 'wait (for)' that govern either the genitive or the accusative. Eventually, the object-marking rule was morphologized, leaving the genitive-accusative as it is today.

This theory, paradoxically, is so appealing that it has never been seriously discussed — only generally acepted (see e.g. Meillet 1934/1965:463, Vaillant 1964:177, Mareš 1967:485–486), or, more rarely, rejected (Andersen 1980:20). Developed mainly by A. I. Thomson in the early years of this century, it remains the only well established theory about the rise of the genitive-accusative and its history in either Russian or other Slavic languages.[3]

The difficulties raised by Thomson's theory derive most obviously from the directness of the connection he assumes between the disambiguation of grammatical relations, on the one hand, and, on the other, the distinctiveness of Russian (or Slavic) case forms. Why should a goal of eliminating subject-object ambiguity lead to a morphological change affecting all accusative case forms, including those, such as prepositional objects, that can never have been confused with nominatives? Why not respond more directly, for example by stabilizing word order — as eventually happened anyway? And if subject-object disambiguation was so important, why does Modern Russian today allow such a high degree of nondifferentiation between subject and object, while still differentiating among different kinds of objects? Does case syncret-ism not contribute, in fact, to a new kind of ambiguity — ambiguity between competing kinds of object, normally distinct in Russian? Finally, assuming that it would have been useful to supplant original accusatives with new, genitive-like forms, how did speakers manage to implement such a salient change in their inflexional system?

Probably the most important problem in treating the genitive-accusative as a response to a problem in coding grammatical relations is how to account for the fully morphological character of the genitive-accusative, which is not syntacti-cally restricted in any way. Nearly all proponents of Thomson's theory have based their arguments on the fact that the genitive-accusative in its early stages affected mainly (although never exclusively) direct objects and not accusative objects of prepositions. This fact has been put to two slightly different uses. First, it is sometimes suggested (see Comrie 1978a) that the genitive-accusative was innovated first, for communicative-functional reasons, and "grammatical-ized" later — that is, the rule acquired certain limitations according to the nature of the language in which it had been innovated, but the motivation for the rule originally had been the need to compensate for a very general communicative problem. It is argued below that this analysis, in which morphologization works to the detriment of communicative functionality, really represents an impover-ished view of morphology; we will examine (Chapter Four) some of the morpho-logical factors that tended to promote and create a functional network for the expansion of the genitive-accusative in Russian noun declension.

The second approach, often not explicitly separated from the first (see Comrie 1978a), is to say that the original syntactic condition on the appearance of the genitive-accusative shows that the genitive-accusative was at first syntactic, not morphological, and became morphological later, thereby acquiring additional conditions that had nothing to do with the original motivation of the rule. I wish to suggest that this interpretation relies on a confusion between the original motivation of a rule and the means by which it is implemented. As has been generally realized, there was of course a connection between the genitive-accusative and syntactic genitive case marking, and, as Meillet (1897:153–163) pointed out, it is often impossible to distinguish genitive case forms from genitive-accusatives. This, as we will see, is because the latter arose precisely through reanalysis of the former; thus, the best environments for the early genitive-accusative were those that marginally permitted syntactic genitive objects as well as accusatives. These environments only marginally included prepositional phrases, because, of all the prepositions, only *za* permitted both accusative and genitive rection (see Meillet 1897:161, *Slovník* 11 [1965]:626). Thus, the restriction to direct-object accusatives can be interpreted as the result of a trivial practical constraint, and need not be evidence of the genitive-accusative's underlying syntactic motivation. We return to this point in Chapters Five and Six.

In general, the functionalist approach has tended to promote a notion of the early genitive-accusative as a syntactic rule introducing a new class of genitive objects where (nominative-) accusatives had previously occurred. This, at least, is the most obvious interpretation of the idea that the genitive-accusative prevented objects from being confused with subjects: if the function of the rule was to obviate confusion, then we expect the dysfunctional forms to be replaced by unambiguous ones before, at least, the new forms enter environments where they can be further confused with genitive-case objects. In fact, however, since the earliest genitive-accusatives were reanalyzed genitive-case objects reinterpreted as accusatives, they did not replace nominative-accusatives *in texts*, but only *in paradigms*, and the textual frequency of genitive or apparently genitive-like forms was probably not increased very much or at all, since genitive rection simply receded gradually in the face of the innovated form (see Chapters Two and Five for fuller discussion). Although such an order of implementation for the genitive-accusative does not show that the functionalist hypothesis must be wrong, it nevertheless weakens it considerably. Specifically, it eliminates the only strictly syntactic evidence supporting the theory that the genitive-accusative originated as a syntactically motivated rule, replacing it, at best, with the possibility that subject-object ambiguity would potentially have been increased, if the disappearing genitive-case objects had not been morphologically reanalyzed, but instead were simply replaced with (nominative-) accusative forms.

In addition to syntactic evidence, Thomson also adduces evidence of, mainly, two other kinds. One sort is typological and comparative: there have been many examples of languages developing means of avoiding syncretism between subject forms and object forms. This may show that it is better to avoid such syncretism than not, but it does not prove that the Slavic genitive-accusative originated and developed mainly (much less exclusively) as a response to subject-object ambiguity. The most interesting sort of evidence supporting the functionalist theory is, characteristically, morphological: the genitive-accusative arose in noun declensions only after they had developed nominative-accusative syncretism, and never developed in noun paradigms that already had a distinct accusative case form. Hence, the argument runs, the genitive-accusative arose quite literally as a response to nominative-accusative syncretism.

This argument, of course, completely ignores the history of the genitive-accusative in pronoun declensions, which developed genitive-accusative syncretism even in paradigms that had previously had a nonsyncretic accusative form. Therefore, on the face of it, Thomson's theory is inadequate to account for the evidence before us, or at least requires separating the pronoun genitive-accusative from the noun genitive-accusative. Actually, however, there is considerable indication that nominative-accusative syncretism actually supported the rise of the genitive-accusative in pronouns as well as in nouns. Thus, this aspect of Thomson's argument — namely, that nominative-accusative syncretism tended to lead to genitive-accusative syncretism — is better founded than at first appears. At the same time, both sorts of syncretism are, after all, inflexional phenomena, and a general tendency to replace one sort by another, while it may suggest that one sort is preferable to another, does not mean that the innovated form originated as a syntactic case marking rule on direct objects. In other words, we can accept Thomson's view that nominative-accusative syncretism is particularly undesirable without agreeing with his suggestion that the genitive-accusative originated as a kind of case marking. In general, the relation between genitive-accusative syncretism and nominative-accusative syncretism is rather complex, and it will be discussed in some detail in Chapter Four. For our present purposes, we may conclude that the functionalist motivation ascribed by Thomson to the rise of the genitive-accusative is probably not so much incorrect as it is just much less important than he thought in providing an overall explanation for the phenomenon he sought to characterize. Moreover, his linking communicative functionality with syntactic as distinct from inflexional status in the grammar of Old

Russian was clearly wrong. There is no reason to believe that there ever was a (syntactic) rule marking animate direct objects with the genitive case.

If, on the contrary, we adopt the view that the genitive-accusative originated as an inflexional phenomenon, we will find fewer anomalies, while the grammatical functioning of the genitive-accusative, if different from what Thomson proposed, is at least as clear, and is probably more interesting, not only historically, but also synchronically.

In fact, a synchronic corollary of the diachronic revision I propose is that the Modern Russian genitive-accusative is about as functional as the genitive-accusative in Old Russian, and functions in roughly the same ways. Moreover, although it is impossible to document the innovation of the genitive-accusative in Slavic (as distinct from its extension in Old Russian), there is no reason to suppose that the motivations for its original innovation were much different from those for its later development. The genitive-accusative, I wish to suggest, is not a morphologized relic of a once functional marker of direct object relations; rather, the role of the genitive-accusative in Modern Russian is essentially what it always has been, and that role is best examined in the context of the history and structure of Russian inflexional morphology, and only afterwards in relation to syntax.

The analysis I propose (presented in detail in the remaining chapters) provides a solution to a problem that has troubled most of the scholars who have studied the origin of the genitive-accusative — namely, how speakers of Common Slavic could have accepted such a radical change in form as the substitution of genitives for accusatives. To a great extent, they never had to, since the genitive-accusative replaced not accusative objects, but genitive ones. Although the underlying reasons for such a change may have had to do with the sort of communicative functioning that Thomson noted, there is little evidence that they did; on the other hand, the historical relation between the receding genitive objects and the advancing genitive-accusative suggests that the spread of genitive-accusative syncretism was a function of change in the Old Russian system of object (transitivity) relations. Such changes are known independently to have occurred. The relation of the genitive-accusative to historical shifts in transitivity in Russian and Old Russian will be described in Chapter Five.

This raises a more general point, having to do with the distinctiveness or nondistinctiveness of the outputs of separate components of the grammar. Even if, as suggested above, the genitive-accusative was never a syntactic rule, its output is nevertheless a genitive-like form, identical with the output of syntactic rules. In addition, because the early genitive-accusative was favored by many of the same conditions that favored the appearance of genitive objects, individual genitive forms are not always clearly of one type to the exclusion of the other, even though the rules presumably generating them apply to different classes of forms and cannot be collapsed. This indeterminacy has troubled most scholars who have studied the history of the genitive-accusative, in the sense that they have often disagreed on which examples belong to which class (see e.g. Lunt 1974:127 on Łoś, and Pennington 1980:313 on Cocron). Yet only Meillet, who was the first to separate the two classes of genitive forms in principle, seems to have been aware that the indeterminacy he observed was inherent in the data, and could not be resolved except arbitrarily. The extent of the overlap is very large; this fact, which has not previously been reported, tends to support the view that reanalysis of genitive verbal objects was the main mechanism through which the genitive-accusative was extended. Thus, the innovation of the genitive-accusative rode "piggy-back" on syntactic genitive case marking, in spite of the fact that the forms in question were rather sharply differentiated semantically (see Chapter Five) and were apparently generated by entirely different grammatical components.

2.2 The Slough of Despond, or Documenting the History of Russian.

The attested history of the Russian genitive-accusative is, of course, subject to the same philological constraints as any other phenomenon of Russian historical grammar; moreover, these constraints make themselves felt particularly keenly, because the genitive-accusative was implemented over a long time period, beginning before the 11th century and ending only in the mid-18th. Obviously, the history of the genitive-accusative can only be established on the basis of a secure understanding of the documentation on which that history rests. For this reason, we will have to include in our discussion below occasionally extensive commentary on the sociolinguistic status of the documents in which the genitive-accusative is attested. (This is particularly true in Chapter Two, which deals with phenomena that are well attested but not previously described in any detail.) It goes without saying that my commentary is not intended as a finished survey of roughly 700 years of Russian and Old Russian writing, but is mainly intended as an aid to readers, who may find it helpful to know my assumptions and opinions about what the relevant documents represent. This is particularly so, because I am obliged by the material to make certain philological distinctions among my sources.

Different kinds of texts use the genitive-accusative differently, and the language of East Slavic religious writing in particular is distinct in this as in so many other ways from the language of, for example, writs and charters. The religious texts are written in a language (hereafter called East Slavonic) that is derived from Old Church Slavonic but developed in East Slavic territory; East Slavonic religious texts were indeed often copies of Slavonic originals or translations made outside the East Slavic area, and generally little change was made in the language of non-East-Slavonic sources. Because this language is not properly East Slavic at all, such texts cannot be treated together with, for example, secular documents of native origin. At the same time, however, the language of these texts has to be taken into account here, because East Slavonic usage is found even in most writing of native authorship, especially in the early chronicle texts. The language of the chronicle texts is, in its turn, controversial, since, in many if not most parts of the chronicles, it seems to be identical with the East Slavonic religious language, but elsewhere (or even simultaneously) it represents East Slavic usage. Unfortunately for the analyst, it is usually impossible to identify any well defined boundary between Slavonic and non-Slavonic passages in the chronicles, and even the status of individual elements as Slavonic or non-Slavonic is difficult to determine (see Shevelov 1968, Hüttl-Worth 1973, Issatschenko 1980). Meanwhile, the language of the writs and charters, which is in general much more distinct from both the chronicles and the religious texts than the latter two are from each other, is no more guaranteed than the other types of writing to represent colloquial East Slavic; in view of the special nature and functions of legal language in general, it is extremely unlikely that it does (see Worth 1975). This rough taxonomy of our documentation will be expanded in later chapters, to include, for example, legal texts of a religious nature, the generally non-literary birchbark letters (which do not, however, provide any new information about the genitive-accusative), and secular personal narratives and other types of writing that proliferated in the later medieval and early modern periods. In general, I have tried to include reasonable coverage of all major types of documentation, but to treat them separately, insofar as they differ with respect to the genitive-accusative.

In general, East Slavonic was much more conducive to the early use of some types of genitive-accusative syncretism than was non-Slavonic East Slavic; this difference is correlated with the use in Slavonic but not non-Slavonic of certain syntactic and lexical constructions where the genitive-accusative is preferred. Insofar as the difference between Slavonic and non-Slavonic can be identified with the availability or unavailability of these formal structures, analysis can operate on just the formal conditions favoring or inhibiting the genitive-accusative, ignoring the fact that these conditions may be met more or less frequently in different kinds of texts. This approach is adequate for a description of the genitive-accusative in a single text or even in a range of roughly contemporary texts, but is inadequate for an historical analysis. The reason is that Slavonic was, for some writers at least, a normative system, and the norms could apparently be deliberately archaizing, were sometimes arbitrary, and were in general unstable over time. For example, it is indisputable that Slavonic texts make relatively frequent use of the genitive-accusative *ego* 'him, it' at a time when this form is exceptional in non-Slavonic texts (see Chapter Two). Nevertheless, once *ego* became common and apparently unrestricted, its nongenitive competitor *i* was apparently considered appropriate and correct in religious texts, where it continued to be used through the 17th century, well after it had disappeared in all other kinds of writing (see Durnovo 1924/1962:270). We even find corrections of *ego* to *i* in 13th- and 14th-century religious writing — the period when *ego* was appearing in non-Slavonic writing, and was becoming a very frequent form in all kinds of texts. In at least one example — number (11) in Chapter Two — the preferred form *i* cannot represent the scribe's normal speech. Examining the history of accusative *ego* without reference to the difference between Slavonic and non-Slavonic writing, we risk misinterpreting early occurrences of accusative *ego* in some chronicle texts (where, as I will show in Chapter Two, §3.2.1.2, it is not a colloquial innovation but is instead a conservative Slavonic element — see also Klenin 1983), as well as failing to account for late retention of *i* in religious texts. Excluding religious texts from the corpus would solve the second problem, but would make the early chronicle usage completely obscure. At the same time, including as many different kinds of text as possible, it is important to take into account their heterogeneous origins and functions, even though they are in some cases, as in the chronicle texts, imprecisely known. I have tried to characterize the documents mentioned below so as to avoid confusion; it should be noted that, throughout, I have used the term "East Slavic" in a very broad sense, to cover all the Slavic texts written or copied in the East Slavic area, including "East Slavonic" ones. Any variations in usage are noted as they occur.

3. On the Purpose and Arrangement of This Book.

As is clear from the preceding discussion, the purpose of this book is not to present an exhaustive analysis of the history of the genitive-accusative, to review everything that is known or has been said about it, or to provide a textbook for an imagined special course. Instead, I have tried to fill certain gaps in our knowledge of the chronological development of the genitive-accusative and to offer a new interpretation of it. I have focused on just the issues that have most interested me, and I have tried to be brief. The reader I have in mind is probably a specialist in Slavic philology or historical grammar, but nonspecialists should be able to read either the whole book or whatever parts of it might interest them.

Parts One and Two can be read independently, although each successive chapter does to some extent build on the preceding one. In Chapters Two and Three, I report on the development of the pronominal genitive-accusatives, generalized before 1400. The main lines of this development are described most fully with respect to the anaphoric pronouns (Chapter Two), which are by far the most abundantly attested. Since most of the data are new, they are presented in considerable detail. Chapter Three covers all the other pronouns, and can be skipped by the reader who is not particularly interested in them. Chapter Four treats the noun and adjective genitive-accusative, whose history is much better studied than that of the pronoun. There has been some controversy over the relationship between the two main types of genitive-accusative, but they are usually considered to have evolved separately within East Slavic. Chapter Four re-examines this question as well as reviewing the history of the noun genitive-accusative itself. Since many of the data are well known (see e.g. Unbegaun 1935, Cocron 1962, Pennington 1980, Sobolevskij 1907/1962, Durnovo 1927, Šaxmatov 1910/1957), they are presented in rather little detail. The main purpose of the chapter is to show the relation of the noun genitive-accusative to other inflexional phenomena, especially the extension of nominative-accusative syncretism to the plural and the loss of plural gender distinctions, and to describe the semantics of the noun genitive-accusative in the pre-modern period.

Whereas Part One is diachronic, Part Two combines synchronic and diachronic approaches, focusing on the correlation between the genitive-accusative and two of the categories of Russian inflexion with which it interacts: case (Chapter Five) and gender (Chapter Six). I do not discuss number, partly because it warrants separate study, and partly because the interaction of animacy with number is less directly related to the general problems to which the rest of the book is devoted. Chapter Five draws heavily on diachronic material, some of which is first introduced in Part One. Chapter Six discusses the status of animacy in the gender system of Modern Russian and re-examines the question of correlating the two main types of genitive-accusative (animacy-marking vs. generalized) with part of speech (noun and adjective vs. pronoun).

I have included in the bibliography most of the items that I have found useful, regardless of whether they are cited directly in the text. However, I have omitted nearly all works about the genitive-accusative in Slavic languages other than Russian, as well as works in which the genitive-accusative is compared to similar phenomena in non-Slavic languages. I have also omitted bibliographic entries for works not available to me directly, although some of them are cited in footnotes, along with locations of published references to them. The list of sources cited in the text does not represent the whole corpus from which I gathered material, since it excludes sources that are not cited at all or are cited through secondary literature.

Finally, it may be noted that the present study is more or less closely related to four of my own articles, all listed in the bibliography. Klenin 1980a is a progress report on some of the material presented more fully in Chapter Four, section 1. Klenin 1980b presents in detail much of the material summarized in the table in Chapter Five, and Klenin 1980c and 1983 are special studies of the genitive-accusative in the Laurentian Manuscript version of the Primary Chronicle, which, for this reason, is not discussed in detail below.

NOTES

1. This statement ignores the problem of deciding which nouns are animate. Usually obvious, the choice is less clear in pairs of examples such as *mertvec* 'dead man, corpse' (animate) and *trup* 'corpse, carcass, dead body' (inanimate).

2. To some extent numbers also belong here, but their usage is idiosyncratic and will not be discussed.

3. The classical theory as presented here is left somewhat less specific than in Thomson's or other formulations of the early 1900's. There was some disagreement over which genitives were to have been the source of the early genitive-accusatives (Delbrück suggesting partitive genitives, Sommer the verbs of perception), and, with the possible exception of Sommer (see Chapter Two §2), no one, including Thomson, was at all clear on the means by which the genitive-accusative was to have been implemented. Thomson apparently considered the genitive-accusative to have derived from partitive objects, but without retaining the partitive meaning, as the result of speakers' mistakes. These mistakes were on such a low level, however, that they were not rejected or misunderstood. According to Thomson, such 'incorrect' genitives would have replaced the 'correct' accusatives at first only when it was necessary to avoid actual ambiguity, but this replacement gradually expanded in range. (See Thomson 1908.) Thomson clearly believed that the genitive-accusative even from its very earliest stages represented a replacement in actual texts or speech situations of old accusative forms in favor of, at first, full-fledged genitives that later were reinterpreted as accusatives with genitive form. It is this very general theory that is addressed in the present book.

PART ONE

Chapter Two. The Anaphoric Pronoun Genitive-Accusative.

1. Introduction.

There is no Slavic writing that antedates the earliest occurrences of anaphoric pronoun genitive-accusative syncretism. The masculine singular genitive-accusative *ego* competes with accusative *i* in the oldest texts, and eventually completely replaced it everywhere in Slavic, except for a few frozen prepositional phrase expressions such as Polish *nań* 'on it' (but compare also *doń* 'to it', where etymologically accusative *ń* appears with the preposition *do*, which governs the genitive). Even such vestiges as these are completely lacking in Russian, which had generalized both masculine singular and plural genitive-accusatives before 1400. The plural genitive-accusative *ix* is very poorly attested in early East Slavic manuscripts (both Slavonic and non-Slavonic) from before 1300; the usual nongenitive accusative was *ja* or *ě*, although other forms occur (see below). The accusatives *ego* and *ix* were generalized more or less at the same time in the 14th century. Dual anaphoric accusatives are not well enough represented in texts to warrant separate discussion. The neuter and feminine genitive-accusatives are attested from the 14th century on, according to Durnovo (1924/1962:270). Earlier examples have sometimes been adduced by other scholars, but most represent genitive objects of transitive verbs under negation.[1] Sobolevskij (1907/1962:201), however, offers the following 12th-century example from the *Skazanie o Borise i Glebe:*[2]

(1) *umysli sъzьdati cьrkъvь i sъzьdavъ jeě*
     'he decided to found a church, and having founded it (gen.-acc.)',

as well as two 14th-century examples:

(2) *nakazavъ jeja*
     'having instructed her'
(3) *bivъ eja*
     'having beat her'

Note that the earliest of the genitive-accusative forms refers to an inanimate object, and all three examples are objects of participial, rather than personal, verb forms; in both respects, the examples above are typical of early anaphoric genitive-accusatives in general. According to Unbegaun (1935:368), the feminine and neuter genitive-accusatives were generalized by the beginning of the

16th century. The feminine accusative *ju* continues to occur as a Slavonicism in later texts (Pennington 1980:245) and is apparently found sporadically even in modern dialects (Avanesov-Orlova 1965:130), but the old neuter accusative has apparently disappeared without trace. The feminine and neuter accusatives will not be discussed further here. In general, the process of losing the old accusatives began in the masculine singular and spread to other numbers and genders only after about 1200 at the earliest. The loss of the old plural form occurred apparently very rapidly, in contrast to the lingering resistance offered by the feminine singular.

There are a number of factors likely to have contributed to the development of the genitive-accusative in anaphoric pronouns. The disappearance of the old accusative *i* may well have been partly induced by the fact that it is an extremely short word, and a realization of an old *$jь$, whose survival would have been made problematical by the vagaries of the Slavic jer shift. Although the jer shift itself was over by the time *i* was lost, the morphological readjustments triggered by the jer shift were still going on (Isačenko 1970). The special vulnerability of *i* is suggested by the fact that, except for a few prepositional phrase locutions, it has disappeared everywhere in Slavic, regardless of the fate of either the other anaphoric accusatives or the animate genitive-accusative. Similar factors may have also hastened the loss of the plural accusative *ě*, discussed in section 3 below.

At the same time, it has been widely, and probably correctly, assumed that the anaphoric genitive-accusative is related to the animate genitive-accusative of noun declension, although the connection is not entirely clear (see Chapter Four). Meillet (1897) suggests that the animate genitive-accusative arose in Common Slavic under the influence of the already existing anaphoric genitive-accusative *ego*; this is unlikely (see Berneker 1904), but, on the other hand, the noun genitive-accusative was well established in East Slavic by the 13th century, and may thus have influenced the later history of the genitive-accusative in anaphoric pronouns. The overwhelming majority of occurrences of the anaphoric pronouns had human antecedents, and it might be suggested (see Timberlake 1974:184) that the anaphoric pronouns were treated as a class of animates on the basis of their normal behavior. However, there is no direct evidence that supports this hypothesis, since in fact the earliest anaphoric genitive-accusatives were disproportionately often inanimate, so that there is no apparent extension from human-referential to other anaphoric accusatives. Such a diachronic extension is not necessarily implied by the anaphoric pronouns as a class enjoying animate or personal-reference status, but there is little other evidence of such status in Old Russian (although see Timberlake 1974:184).

The chronology of the anaphoric genitive-accusative was quite different from that of the corresponding development in nouns (see Chapter Four): by the end of the 14th century, both masculine singular and plural anaphoric pronouns had generalized the genitive-accusative, whereas the noun genitive-accusative was at that time still largely restricted to nouns of human reference, and, within that group, to the singular. The relative speed of the anaphoric development may have resulted partly from its being a replacement of just a small number of forms, as opposed to the more general noun and adjectival syncretism. For whatever reasons, however, the anaphoric development was in some ways quite different from animacy marking, and observations about one of these kinds of syncretism cannot a priori be assumed to apply to the other. For similar kinds of reasons, discussed in the next chapter, neither animacy marking nor the anaphoric genitive-accusative can be treated entirely together with genitive-accusative syncretism in personal and other pronouns. In this chapter, we will discuss only the anaphoric genitive-accusative, and in Chapters Four and Five we will return to some of the ways in which the various classes of genitive-accusative are alike in spite of their differences.

The genitive-accusatives *ego, ix,* and (dual) *eju* are attested in the following East Slavic and East Slavonic documents from before 1400 (listed in chronological order by date of copying), which are the source of all the examples discussed in this chapter:

1. Ostromir Gospel of 1056
2. Izbornik of 1076
3. Arxangel Gospel of 1092
4. Sinajskij Paterik, 11th or 12th century
5. Vygoleksinskij Sbornik (late 12th century, according to Golyšenko 1977:10)
6. Uspenskij Sbornik (12th–13th century, according to Knjazevskaja 1971:25)
7. Life of Nifont in the longer redaction (1219)
8. Life of Savva the Enlightened (13th century — see Vinogradov 1968:137)
9. Smolensk trade treaties (1223–1300)
10. Novgorod treaty with Jaroslav Jaroslavič (1270)
11. Russkaja Pravda in the Synod text of 1282 (Novgorod Nomocanon)
12. Novgorod writs and charters (early 14th century)
13. First Novgorod Chronicle in the Synod Manuscript (1330–1350 and possibly 13th century — see §3.1.1)
14. Birchbark letters #5 (1340–1369) and #314 (after 1369)
15. Other legal texts (14th century)
16. Primary Chronicle and Suzdal Chronicle, in the Laurentian Manuscript of 1377.

The corpus from which the attestations are drawn includes all the known legal texts from this period, as well as all the published birchbarks (see "Primary Sources"). The chronicles listed are the only ones extant from the relevant period. On the other hand, the early religious texts have not all been exhaustively analyzed, and any additional documentation of the genitive-accusative will therefore be found in religious texts. I have encountered no religious texts from this period that both contained a large number of anaphoric pronouns and did not contain at least some genitive-accusatives. As would be expected from the preponderance of religious texts in the materials that are available (see Sobolevskij 1907/1962:1–18), nearly all the attestations from the first two and a half centuries are in religious writing. The language of these texts, which in the last chapter I dubbed 'East Slavonic', stood at different times and places in varying relations to native East Slavic, and in the so-called 'mixed' texts, such as the chronicles, Slavonic and non-Slavonic elements occur side by side. I will argue in §3 that the genitive-accusatives in the chronicle manuscripts at first originated mainly in Slavonic texts, since in large and fairly well-defined segments of the chronicles the genitive-accusatives occur only in markedly Slavonic environments, which are characterized below, and nearly entirely in the singular — a statistical feature of religious-text usage (see §2). I will show how certain features of specifically Slavonic writing facilitate the rise of the genitive-accusative, and I will discuss syntactic and lexical semantic conditions favoring the use of *ego* over *i* in texts where both forms occur.

I will also show, however, that the chronicle texts are not uniform in their distribution of anaphoric genitive-accusatives. There is great variation in the frequency of the genitive-accusatives, as well as in the restrictions on their appearance. In general, parts of the chronicle texts with frequent use of *ix* as well as *ego* do not restrict either form to Slavonic or other identifiable environments. In the Laurentian manuscript, the division between the more and the less restricted use of the genitive-accusatives corresponds to the geographical focus of the narrative: southern narrative does not in general use the genitive-accusative outside of apparent quotations from religious literature, whereas narrative set in the north makes extensive use of particularly the plural genitive-accusative. The large number of examples involved (about 968 in both chronicle manuscripts) makes it very unlikely that this skewed distribution is due to chance; it most plausibly can be attributed to the influence of the chronicles' source texts. In the Novgorod Chronicle manuscript, the variation in usage is apparently time dependent, rather than geographic. In both our chronicle manuscripts, the main influences on the use of *ego* — Slavonic vs. non-Slavonic and northern vs. southern usage, as well as statistical increase across time — must have been influential already within the sources of our extant manuscripts, and were not demonstrably within the conscious control of the scribes of the preserved (14th century) texts.

The legal texts' usage tends to show that the anaphoric genitive-accusative is very unlikely to have been an exclusively Slavonic feature in 13th-century Smolensk or Novgorod; this, in general, confirms the pattern of the Novgorod Chronicle and the northern narrative of the Suzdal Chronicle. As shown in §4, however, the legal texts are a difficult source to use for present purposes. Of even less direct use are the birchbark letters, which contain examples of the anaphoric genitive-accusative beginning only in the mid-14th century. The birchbark letters will not be discussed further in this chapter.

2. The accusative *ego/ix* in East Slavic religious texts.

The anaphoric genitive-accusative *ego* occurs in East Slavic religious texts of the 11th to 13th centuries, well before it is attested in other kinds of East Slavic writing. The masculine singular direct object *ego* is proportionately much better attested than the prepositional object *nego*, but both are found in texts throughout the period in question. The plural *ix* is poorly attested; there are some apparent examples, but none that are completely clear. Vostokov (1843) noted accusative *ego* in the word-register to his edition of the Ostromir Gospel of 1056, citing the following example:

(4)   *otъvěščavъ ijuda prědajęi jego*
      'Judas who betrayed him answered' (Mt. 26.25; Ostr. 158c)

Genitive-accusative *nego* also occurs in Ostromir, as in the following example:

(5)   *da vsakъ věroujęi vъ nego ne pogybnetь*
      'that anyone believing in him shall not perish' (J. 3.16; Ostr. 12c)

Other examples also occur in Ostromir. A repeated phrase may show the genitive-accusative in one occurrence and the nongenitive form in another. For example, beside (5) above, Ostromir (12d; J. 3.18) also has *věrouęi vъ nь* 'believing in him', with nongenitive accusative *nь*. Other 11th-century attestations are found in the Izbornik of 1076 and the Arxangel Gospel of 1092:

(6)   *progněva sę oubo na nego g(ospod)ь*
      'and the Lord got angry at him' (Izb. 1076, leaf 221.3, page 591)

(7)   *tou raspęša jego*
      'here they crucified him' (Arx. 110, L. 23.33; cited from Gribble 1973:54)

(8)   *mъnozi věrovaša vъ nego*
      'many believed in him' (Arx., no leaf cited, J. 4.39;
      cited from Vondrák 1925: 182)

(9)   *jako da oubiti jego*
      'how to kill him' (Arx. 116, Mt. 27.1; Gribble 1973: 54)

One genitive-accusative *jego* in the Izbornik of 1076 was corrected to *i* by a later (14th-century?) scribe:

(10)   *čьto trěboujetь otъ nasъ b(og)ъ ... xvaly li nъ xvalętь jego angely*
       'What does God require of us? Praise? But the angels praise him.'[3]
       (13.7–10, page 175)

Because of its late date, the correction must be artificial, as are a number of other corrections made by the same scribes or near contemporaries; for example, another correction in the passage above is the insertion of a titlo over the word *angely*, which is not an abbreviation and therefore does not require a titlo. Even more telling is the correction to *i* of a syntactic genitive *jego*, object of a negated verb, where the scribe making the correction cannot have had *i* in his own speech:

(11)   *gore lěnivumou. iskati vo* (!, EK) *imatь tъgda. iže budetь*
       zъlě izgoubilъ. nъ ne obręštetь jego (corrected to *i*).
       'Woe to the indolent, for he will then seek whom he evilly ruined,
       but will not find him'. (79v 5–8, page 308)

These corrections all date from after 1300, many from the 15th century and later, when *i* had been displaced by *ego* in East Slavic; apparently, the East Slavonic norms shifted in favor of the older, colloquially now lost, form, and *ego* came to be perceived as an innovation, because it was colloquially normal.

The Vygoleksinskij Sbornik (late 12th or 13th century) contains numerous attestations, including the following ones:

(12)   *povelěvъ ... krěpъcě že jego zatvoriti*
       'having ordered [them] ... to shut him up firmly' (122v, 7–10)
(13)   *privede bl(a)gago mouža önogo jego že*
       bě posъlalъ i bijetь jego predъ zъlodějemъ
       'he brought that good man whom he had sent and
       beats him before the evildoer' (129v, 16 – 130a, 1)
(14)   *prizyvaxou bo ixъ*
       'for they called them' (118v, 12–13)

However, many of the attestations in the Vygoleksinskij Sbornik are unclear.

The Uspenskij Sbornik, from the 12th or early 13th century, contains numerous attestations of *ego/ix*, nearly all singular direct objects. Among examples of *ego* and *ix* are the following ones:

(15)   *da jego pogoubętь*
       'that they condemn him' (200a, 25–26)
(16)   *sъvětъ sъtvoriste na njego*
       'you have held a council against him' (200c, 27–28)
(17)   *stavlęaxou jego pisati*
       'they made him write' (201b, 14–15)

The Life of Nifont, copied in 1219, also shows accusative *ego* and *ix*, as is illustrated by the following examples:

(18) *pokaži mi jego*
'show him to me' (page 264, 33)
(19) *xotę oubiti jego*
'wanting to kill him' (page 278, 24)
(20) *pomiloui jego*
'have mercy on him' (page 305, 10)

Finally, probably the youngest of the manuscripts dealt with here, the 13th-century Life of Savva the Enlightened, contains many examples, including the following ones:

(21) *starecь že bl(a)g(oslo)vivъ jego oučaše i*
'the monk blessing him instructed him' (page 349, 19–20)
(22) *i ješče byvъšamъ na nego klętvamъ*
'there still being curses on him' (page 155, 1–2)

Examples (4) through (22) above show that the genitive-accusative *ego* occurs in East Slavic religious texts from 1056 through the 13th century. I know of no religious texts from this period containing a large number of anaphoric accusatives that do not contain at least some occurrences of accusative *ego*.

The frequency of the genitive-accusative in the texts cited varies widely, and there is no simple correlation of frequency with time of writing. The Uspenskij Sbornik, for example, restricts the genitive-accusative nearly entirely to singular direct objects, where it accounts for about 12% of all possible occurrences. The Izbornik of 1076, on the other hand, uses both direct-object *ego* and prepositional-object *nego* in about 40% of all possible occurrences, and the direct-object form is proportionately far commoner than the prepositional object. (The Izbornik has about 21 occurrences of *ego* and *nego*, out of a possible 53. The Uspenskij Sbornik contains about 68 occurrences of *ego* out of a possible 563, and the entire Sbornik contains only one occurrence of *nego*.)[4] The Uspenskij Sbornik is generally considered a very conservative manuscript, and although the usual dating places it a century or more later than the Izbornik of 1076, its restricted use of the genitive-accusative corresponds to a general conservatism of orthography and language. Similarly, the first scribe of the 13th-century Life of Savva the Enlightened is believed to have been writing at the same time as the manuscript's other two scribes, but he was much more conservative than they (see Vinogradov 1968:165). The first scribe used *ego* 21 times out of a possible 73 (29%), whereas in the rest of the manuscript *ego* occurs 23 times out of 37 (about 62%). Thus, the Life of Savva uses accusative *ego* on the average about 40% of the time, the same proportion as in the Izbornik of 1076, but the generally more innovative part of the later text uses the genitive-accusative much more frequently. The numbers involved, of course, are rather small, but the variation is still substantial. It is particularly striking in the case of the Life of Savva, presumably a fairly homogeneous text, where, for that reason, the differences in usage cannot be ascribed to variation in different source texts. The situation is naturally more complicated in texts compiled from heterogeneous sources, as we will see in our discussion of the Novgorod Chronicle in the Synod Manuscript (§3 below).

The distribution in religious texts of accusative *ego* (and *ix*, to the extent that it occurs at all) is in principle indistinguishable from Old Church Slavonic usage, as described by Meillet (1897), Grünenthal (1910:358–359), Vaillant (1964:176–180), Lunt (1974:46, 126–127), and others (see below). In addition, as is shown in §3, accusative *ego* in the earlier parts of the chronicle texts is specifically a Slavonic variant, and *ego* is not attested at all outside of religious texts before 1223 (see §4). It may be tempting to see accusative *ego* as a borrowing from Old Church Slavonic into East Slavonic and thence to East Slavic in general. However, it is likely that accusative *ego* was not borrowed, at least individually, but was favored by factors present in Old Church Slavonic and East Slavonic, but apparently lacking in non-Slavonic East Slavic.

One element very likely to have been important is the presence in Slavonic (but not non-Slavonic) of the relative pronoun *iže*, whose declension was nearly identical to that of anaphoric *i*. The declension of relative and anaphoric pronouns differs in only two ways: first, the presence of the particle *že* following the declined part of the relative pronoun, and, second, the lack of a nominative anaphoric form, parallel to the *iže, jaže, eže*, and so on of the relative. In the masculine singular, the form *iže* occurs as both nominative and accusative, but, as an accusative, *iže* competes with the form *egože* (identical, of course, with the genitive). The accusative *egože* is in fact so common that Grünenthal (1910:358) treats it as the only possible Old Church Slavonic accusative of *iže*. Although this is not quite true for Old Church Slavonic (see e.g. the Sinai Psalter, 6.1 page 6 in Severʼjanov 1922/1954), it is true that *egože* was common in Old Church Slavonic texts where anaphoric accusative *ego* was rare or lacking. Moreover, accusative *egože* was eventually generalized in East Slavonic texts where *ego* was still exceptional. Thus, Slavonic, but not non-Slavonic East Slavic, had genitive-accusative *egože* as a model supporting the spread of genitive-accusative *ego*.

The reasons for *egože* becoming the preferred accusative in the relative paradigm have not been studied, but it is likely that the pre-existing nominative-accusative syncretism of relative *iže* was an important factor. As already noted in the previous chapter (and discussed more fully in Chapter Four), nominative-accusative syncretism was a prerequisite for developing genitive-accusative syncretism in nouns, and this condition remained in effect at each stage of the extension of the nominal genitive-accusative. The early displacement of accusative *iže* by *egože* suggests that the same condition is found in the early history of the pronoun genitive-accusative. Relative-pronoun genitive-accusative syncretism thus provides a kind of missing link between nominal and anaphoric genitive-accusative syncretism. In the next chapter, we will see that the personal pronouns apparently also make ephemeral use of a nominative-accusative syncretism condition on the genitive-accusative, since the first paradigm to lose its old accusative in favor of the genitive-accusative was probably the second-person plural, which was the only nominative-accusative syncretic paradigm among the personal pronouns.

Even in the oldest East Slavonic religious texts, the anaphoric genitive-accusative is a morphological phenomenon, lacking precise syntactic conditions. In the Ostromir Gospel, for example, the anaphoric genitive-accusative occurs in a variety of environments: direct object of a participial form, as in (4) above, object of a preposition, as in (5), direct object of a main-clause verb, and object of personal verb forms in subordinate clauses, as in the following examples:

(23) *moljaaxǫ jego*
      'they besought him' (Ostr. 32c; J. 4.40)
(24) *iže posъla jego*
      'who sent him' (Ostr. 13c; J. 5.23)

However, certain aspects of the statistical distribution of *ego* in these texts suggest vestigial connections with syntactically conditioned genitive case forms.

According to Vaillant (1964:179), accusative *ego* at first appears in Old Church Slavonic as the direct object of long-form present active participles, although this distribution is not evident in less conservative manuscripts, such as the Savvina Kniga. The same tendency can be observed also in East Slavic, although less clearly, since *ego* had spread into virtually every other type of construction as well. Nevertheless, the genitive-accusative is disproportionately represented in participial constructions even in relatively late texts, including original East Slavic texts such as the Primary Chronicle and Suzdal Chronicle of the Laurentian Manuscript. There is a similar tendency for the genitive-accusative to appear disproportionately often in various sorts of complex object constructions, e.g.

(25) *viděxъ ounyla ... jego zělo*
      'I saw that he was very sad' (Nifont, pages 372.35–373.1)

There are no completely satisfactory explanations for this distribution, but several possibilities present themselves.

First, the tendency for *ego* to appear in subordinate clauses may be a result of its having developed by analogy to *egože*; that is, anaphoric *ego* began appearing first in the environments most like the environments in which we find *egože* — relative clauses and, by extension, other subordinate constructions. The noun genitive-accusatives do not follow such a pattern of extension from subordinate to main clauses, so that this pattern requires an explanation specific to the pronouns; analogy to *egože* is such an explanation.

At the same time, it is possible, although the possibility is both remote and completely speculative, that normal verbal (accusative) rection was weakened in favor of substantival (genitive) rection after substantivized participles — which are by far the commonest participles to take direct objects in East Slavonic texts. Such a confusion occurs sporadically in Latin (Wackernagel 1926/1957:1:291) and is well known in Greek (Goodwin 1930:329), but outside of the possibility raised here it is not known in Slavic. The closest equivalent is genitive rection of supines in early Slavic, and genitive infinitival rection, which is historically derived from the supine usage. The reverse phenomenon, namely deverbal nouns governing the accusative, is noted for Old Church Slavonic by Meillet (1897:161). One clearly cannot posit genitive government for participles entirely for the purpose of deriving genitive-accusatives from them by reanalysis; however, it is not beyond the realm of possibility to suppose that, if nonpersonal verb forms have some tendency in general toward idiosyncratic patterns of rection (and there is some evidence, just noted, that this is so), then this general rectional weakness may have provided an easy point of entry for new genitive-like forms, where accusatives would have been normal.

Such a confluence of syntactic and morphological factors easing the growth of the genitive-accusative is more clearly at work in other ways, where the history of the anaphoric genitive-accusative follows a pattern shared with other classes of genitive-accusative as well. This pattern is the tendency for the earliest genitive-accusatives to occur in environments in which syntactically conditioned genitives are known to have been at least marginally possible. The question that naturally arises is whether such

forms ought to be analyzed as genitive-accusatives at all. The answer is not
always clear in individual examples, but the overall pattern tends strongly
to support the view that the forms in question could not have been produced if genitive-accusative case syncretism had not already begun to
occur.

The basis of the problem is that, just as the genitive-accusative had syntactic conditions, syntactic genitives were conditioned not only by specifications on verbs or on predicates as a whole, but also by specifications on
objects. As Sommer (1916) observed, probably the most directly relevant
genitive-case usage was found with verbs of perception, in particular verbs
of hearing, which in Indoeuropean historically governed accusatives of
inanimate objects and genitive of persons. In Slavic, this usage was
expanded to include verbs of visual perception, such as *zьrěti* and *sъmotriti*,
which regularly governed the genitive. Thus, there were apparent historical
antecedents for variation between genitive and accusative case direct objects depending on the referential animacy of the object, and the variable
rection of verbs of perception seems to have been at first accepted into
Slavic, to judge from its expansion to verbs of visual perception. Sommer
believed that the verbs of perception were the direct syntactic source of the
genitive-accusative, because they governed genitive personal objects but
accusative inanimates; however, although perfectly reasonable, Sommer's
hypothesis lacks direct evidence, since the conditioned choice of genitive or
accusative had been replaced in prehistoric Slavic by a general albeit unstable tendency toward genitive rection by verbs of perception. There is no
evidence within Slavic of animacy or personal reference conditioning these
verbs' rection, but, on the other hand, there probably could not be, because
of interference from the inchoate genitive-accusative.

In addition to the genitive with verbs of perception, Slavic also made
extensive use of genitive rection derived from other sources — for example,
partitive genitives and genitives of negated verbs. All of these genitives were
also partly conditioned by referential features of the case-marked object.
The relation of these other genitives to the genitive-accusative will be discussed separately in Chapter Five. Here, however, we will examine the status of the genitive-accusative *ego* as a direct object of the verb of perception
viděti 'to see' in my Old Russian corpus. The analytical problems raised by
viděti are also raised by a number of other verbs, not only verbs of perception but also other kinds of verbs that in principle permit genitive rection;
however, *viděti* is especially important, since, on the one hand, it is generally agreed to have occasionally governed the genitive in Old Church Slavonic, and, on the other hand, occurrences with *viděti* account for about

9% of my early examples of genitive-accusative *ego*. Why should these examples not be treated as syntactic genitives?

One answer is based on the absolute rarity of *viděti* with the genitive. Leaving aside my own corpus, where it does not occur at all (not counting, of course, the genitive-accusative examples), we may note that there are probably fewer than a dozen examples in all of Old Church Slavonic; about five occur in Suprasliensis (most within a space of two pages), where the verb *viděti* is attested altogether about 630 times (Meyer 1935:27–28). The *Slovník jazyka staroslověnského* (4[1961]:188) notes the rarity of the genitive with *viděti* and offers the following example from the Sinai Psalter (repeated also in the Codex Pogodinianus, 12th century, and the Codex Bononiensis, 13th century):

(26) *xrani nezъlobǫ ï viždь pravoty*
       'preserve innocence and behold righteousness' (*Psalms* 36, 37)

About 10 other examples are cited by Miklosich (1883:4:492), Meillet (1897:158–159), Xodova (1963:60), and Večerka (1963:214). Of these examples, three, including (26) above, show *viděti* in the imperative, and in all the others the verb governs a double object, as in the following examples:

(27) *vъsi divlěxǫ sę viděšte dǫba oblistvъněvъša. ti bo věděěxǫ i izdavъna souxъ*
       'All were astonished, seeing that the oak had borne leaves, for they
       had known it to be long since dry' (Supr., page 18, 16–18)
(28) *Vidite paky vъvrъžena nevoda*
       'you see again that a net has been cast' (Supr., page 127, 27–28)
(29) *Viděxъ dyma iž neǫ do nyněšьnjago vъsxodęšta i zemjǫ
       ognemъ oupepelenǫ. i vsego ploda prazdъna*
       'I saw smoke rising from it (the land) to the present, and the land made
       ashen by fire and all fruit sterile.' (Supr., page 128, 19 seq.)

In all these examples, the verb *viděti* denotes not just visual perception, but also the act of making an observation; for example, in (27) above, the people did not merely see a green oak, but rather noted that the oak was green — hence their astonishment. This nonstative meaning of *viděti* in examples (26) – (29) above unites them with the imperative occurrences of *viděti* noted above, as well as with the use of *viděti* as a perfective verb as noted by Dostál (1954:138). In its sense of 'observing', rather than merely 'having the power of sight', *viděti* is closely synonymous with the much less common and more specialized verbs *zъrěti* and *sъmotriti*, both of which take the genitive. (All three verbs were used to translate most of the same Greek verbs of visual perception, although their relative distribution reflects the semantic differences indicated here.) Thus, it is quite likely that the genitive with *viděti* occurs partly as a result of the influence of verbs regularly

governing the genitive, when *viděti* is being used in a way particularly close
to the meanings of these verbs. In addition, Meillet (1897:158) comments
on the etymological connection of *viděti* with *věděti* 'to know', pointing out
that cognate verbs meaning 'to know' in other Indoeuropean languages
may take the genitive (of inanimate objects). However, regardless of the
validity of these various influences, they were nevertheless in combination
still not strong enough to trigger genitive rection with *viděti* in more than a
handful of instances. In particular, as has often been observed, the genitives
in (26) above actually occur parallel with accusative objects of *viděti*, and,
in general, as noted by Meillet, genitive rection occurred with normally
accusative-governing verbs such as *viděti* nearly entirely with objects belonging to form classes already in the process of developing genitive-
accusative syncretism. (An exception to this rule is (26) above.)[5] Although
forms such as *dǫba* in (27) above are obviously not referentially animate, it
must be kept in mind (see Vaillant 1964:177) that referential restrictions on
the genitive-accusative in Old Church Slavonic were not nearly so rigid as
in later Slavic, and inanimate genitive-accusatives — even neuters — are far
more common than is generally realized. For this reason, *dǫba* in (27) and
the disputed forms in the other examples are marginally possible genitive-
accusatives, just on the basis of their form class; if, of course, these forms
were *not* marginal as genitive-accusatives, there would be no evidence at all,
except for (26) above, that *viděti* ever governed the genitive case. In Old
Church Slavonic, in fact, there is no evidence that *viděti* regularly governed
the genitive, and, to the extent that genitive objects occur with *viděti*, their
acceptability was apparently enhanced by homonymy with genitive-accusatives. Thus, the forms in question are marginal both as genitives and as
genitive-accusatives, although clearly they must be at least one or the other;
we have seen here that, in some sense, they were probably both. Data such
as this led Meillet to conclude that, although the genitive-accusative and
syntactically conditioned genitives were in principle to be distinguished
from each other, nevertheless, the membership of each class is not well
defined. Such indeterminacy characterizes occurrences of *ego* in my corpus
not only with *viděti* but also with other verbs, notably verbs built on the
root *-dad-* 'give' (for example, *vъdati, prědati*), verbs in *-im-* 'take, grasp'
(*poim-, izъm-, vъzъm-*), the verb *(po)běditi* 'to conquer, win over', and various verbs meaning 'to ask' (*vъprositi, vъprašati, ouprašati, moliti*),[6] as well
as in sentences containing negated elements other than the verb, which
normally conditions the genitive when negated; see, for example, (26) above,
and examples in Klenin 1983. However, the indeterminacy of the East Slavonic material is considerably reduced, compared with Old Church Slavonic,

because the verbs in question have lost all traces of genitive rection, except if we consider the occurrences of *ego* to be genitive. Once again taking *viděti* as an example, we may note that in my corpus this very common verb occurs often with *ego* but never with an unambiguous genitive object; moreover, *ego* occurs with all forms of *viděti*, in all kinds of object constructions, and without apparent restrictions on the sense in which *viděti* is being used. Thus *ego* with *viděti* in Old Russian does not fit the Old Church Slavonic restrictions on *viděti*'s genitive objects. Even if an example of a genitive object should be found, it would still have to be explained why, if *ego* is treated as a genitive case object, other objects are regularly in the accusative, whereas the anaphoric pronoun appears normally in the genitive. To the extent that religious texts in my corpus represent copies of older and possibly non-East Slavic materials, it is always possible that *ego* appeared in the original source texts at least partly as a result of the influence of syntactic genitives; however, the occurrences of *ego* in my corpus must have been retained there because they were acceptable genitive-accusatives, presumably supported by the presence both of other genitive-accusatives such as the demonstrative pronouns (see Chapter Three) and of genitive objects of other verbs.

From the preceding discussion, it can be concluded that the marginal examples of *ego* in my corpus are best analyzed as genitive-accusatives, in spite of their being governed by verbs that historically have governed the genitive case. It is clear, however, that there was intense interaction between syntactic and morphological motivations for the appearance of these forms. In Chapter One, this interaction was characterized as reanalysis, but it should be kept in mind that there is little reason to posit a clear linear development from syntactic to morphological status for the genitive forms being discussed here. Thus, for example, genitive rection for *viděti* seems to have been an ephemeral phenomenon within Old Church Slavonic, perhaps competing directly with the simultaneous innovation of the genitive-accusative; at the same time, the disproportionate occurrence of the genitive-accusative with *viděti* and the other verbs mentioned above is not restricted to just the period before 1300, but instead shows up later, for example in the extension of the genitive-accusative to plural nouns. Clearly the genitive-accusative eroded the potential for using various kinds of syntactic genitive objects in East Slavic; thus, syntactic genitive objects of all kinds (partitives, genitives under negation, genitives conditioned by lexical specifications of verbs) have receded farthest in standard Russian, which has a fully stabilized genitive-accusative, whereas Ukrainian makes more use of genitive objects, but uses the genitive-accusative less. (In that sense, all the genitive objects behave as a single class, and the quarrel over which genitives were the source of the genitive-accusative is a discussion of a nonissue: *all* the genitive objects fed the new syncretism.) However, the original system of genitive/accusative transitivity in Slavic, eventually lost through morphological reanalysis (see Chapter Five), does not seem to have been particularly clear in even the earliest texts. On the contrary, the potential variability of genitive and accusative rection in Slavic has apparently been unstable throughout its history, and this instability probably aided the expansion of the genitive-accusative. We return to this point in Chapter Five.

With respect, specifically, to the East Slavonic religious texts' use of *ego*, we may conclude that Old Russian usage was a direct continuation of Old Church Slavonic. Although the frequency of occurrence of the anaphoric genitive-accusative increased over time, vestiges of some Old Church Slavonic constraints on the genitive-accusative can be found in East Slavonic through the 13th century. Throughout this period, the anaphoric genitive-accusative is nearly entirely restricted to the singular, where, however, it is in some texts commoner than the old nongenitive accusative form. Both direct- and prepositional-object genitive-accusatives occur throughout the early period of East Slavonic writing, as they did also in Old Church Slavonic. The distribution of the East Slavic anaphoric genitive-accusatives shows clear signs of originating in the reanalysis of syntactically conditioned genitive forms.

*3. Accusative **ego** and **ix** in the early chronicle texts.*

The chronicle texts in my corpus are the Synod Manuscript of the First Novgorod Chronicle and the Laurentian Manuscript, containing the oldest extant copy of the Primary Chronicle and its continuation, known as the Suzdal Chronicle. These are the oldest East Slavic chronicle texts; both *i* and *ego* are also attested in later chronicle manuscripts, where *i* is obviously a retention of usage in source texts. For example, the late–15th-century Radziwill Manuscript, containing a copy of roughly the same text as the Laurentian Manuscript up to 1206, normally replaces the Laurentian text's *i* with *ego*, but may also drop the *i* altogether or reinterpret it as the homographic conjunction *i* 'and'. The occasional occurrences of *i* remaining in the Radziwill can obviously offer no information about contemporary speech, where *ego* had long since been generalized as the accusative form.

*3.1 Description of the sources and their statistical distribution of the
anaphoric genitive-accusative.*

3.1.1 The Synod Manuscript of the First Novgorod Chronicle. The Synod
Manuscript was copied mainly by three scribes. Additions by several later
scribes will be ignored here. At least one of the three main scribes was writing
as late as 1330, the date of his last entry. He copied leaves 119 through 166, and
the other two scribes wrote, respectively, leaves 1 through 61 (covering events
from 1016/6524 to 1200/6708) and leaves 61 through 118 (from 1200 to
1234/6742). The first two hands are generally believed to be 13th century (see
Dietze 1975:23 and references therein), but Sobolevskij (1907/1962:10) and
Šaxmatov (1938/1968:128) considered them probably contemporary with the
third hand and therefore 14th century. One reason Šaxmatov gives for his
opinion is that the third hand takes up the narrative from the second hand in
midsentence (as does the second hand from the first), so that the successive
hands are not additions, like the work of the fourth and later scribes, to
previously complete works. The third hand, therefore, must either be contemporary with the second hand, or else represent a substitution for a section of
the text that has been lost. (Since the third hand starts a fresh leaf, this would
be mechanically possible.) Dietze reviews the paleographic features distinguishing the third hand from its two predecessors, and he also mentions some
linguistic features that he feels support a bipartite division between the first
two hands and the third. One feature cited by Dietze is the distribution of
anaphoric genitive-accusatives, which, as he points out, are proportionately
much commoner in the work of the third scribe than in that of the second (see
Table 2–1 for details). Dietze fails to note, however, that there is no sudden
break between the second and third scribes' usage. Although it is true that the
second scribe uses *ego/ix* only about half as much as the third scribe, it is also
true that he uses these forms about 10 times as much as the first scribe, who
was writing at the same time that he was. In the main narrative of the
chronicle, accusative *ego/ix* becomes frequent toward the end of the second
scribe's text (leaves 103 to 117, events from 1227/6735 to 1233/6741), and this
part of the second scribe's work shows roughly the same distribution as in the
third scribe's section. This pattern suggests that the use of *ego/ix* depends on
source texts, and not just on the scribes of our extant manuscript. This
impression is strengthened by the fact that *ego* and *ix* are especially common in
two text segments not part of the main narrative but included in the work of
the second scribe. These segments are the story of the capture of Constantinople by the Crusaders (leaves 64 to 72, s.a. 1204/6712) and the story of the Tatar
invasion (leaves 95v to 99v, s.a. 1224/6732). Here, *ego* and *ix* account for
about 40% of masculine singular and plural anaphoric accusatives — as high

Table 2–1

Singular and plural anaphoric accusative forms in the Synod Manuscript (Novgorod Chronicle) and the Laurentian Manuscript (Primary Chronicle and Suzdal Chronicle): the genitive-accusative as a proportion of the total number of accusative singular and plural forms.

	SINGULAR	PLURAL
SYNOD MS. OF THE NOVGOROD CHRONICLE		
1st scribe	1/ 44 (2%)	0/20
2nd scribe	9/ 42 (21%)	6/38 (16%)
3rd scribe	12/ 43 (28%)	17/36 (47%)
	22/129 (17%)	23/94 (24%)
LAURENTIAN MS.		
Primary Chronicle		
1st scribe	2/ 58 (3%)	2/ 57 (3.5%)
2nd scribe	15/200 (7.5%)	2/ 39 (5%)
Suzdal Chronicle		
Part 1	11/104 (11%)	1/ 18 (6%)
Part 2	23/ 80 (29%)	21/ 42 (50%)
Part 3	10/ 91 (11%)	9/ 32 (28%)
	61/533 (11%)	35/188 (19%)

Prepositional-object accusatives are included for all categories, although the prepositional-object genitive-accusative occurs only in some chronicle texts and not in others.

Subdivisions of the Suzdal Chronicle are purely mechanical; each of Parts 1, 2, and 3 contains 1/3 of all the forms being counted — above, 122 or 123 out of the 367 singular and plural anaphoric masculine accusative pronouns.

a proportion as in the work of the third scribe. (The small number of examples in the tales, however, makes the figure much less reliable than the figures for the third scribe's work.) Here, again, the variation from the second scribe's norm can plausibly be attributed to variation in his sources. Alternatively, of course, the passages with frequent occurrences of accusative *ego* and *ix* may provide a better environment for the genitive-accusative than other text segments do. The internal evidence of the Synod Manuscript does not clearly support one of these alternatives over the other, and they need not even be mutually exclusive. It is impossible, however, to show that the Synod Manuscript's distribution of accusative *ego* and *ix* depends on the preferences of the extant manuscript's scribes, or to show that the third scribe's usage differed from that of the other two more than that of the first two scribes differed from each other. In addition, even if such a demonstration were possible, there would still be no way to show that the third scribe must have been working later than the other two, because, as we have seen (§2), there is considerable variation in the frequency of the anaphoric genitive-accusative even in fairly homogeneous texts copied by different scribes working at the same time.

3.1.2 The Laurentian Manuscript of 1377.

The Laurentian Manuscript of 1377 is longer than the Synod Manuscript and contains over 3 times as many examples of anaphoric masculine singular and plural accusatives. Two scribes worked on the Laurentian Manuscript, the first scribe copying the first 40 leaves, up to the year 988/6496. The second scribe, Lavrentij, copied the rest of the Primary Chronicle (up to the year 1110/6618) and the Suzdal Chronicle. (A third scribe apparently also worked on the manuscript; see Proxorov 1972 and annotations in Karskij's edition of the Laurentian Manuscript. The distribution of the genitive-accusative is not substantially affected by this, however.) Like the Synod Manuscript, the Laurentian Manuscript uses *ego* and *ix* as accusatives much more in some places than in others; here, the variation is clearly independent of the personal preferences of the copyists. The first scribe uses genitive-accusative *ego* marginally less often than does Lavrentij in the Primary Chronicle. In the Suzdal Chronicle up to about 1170, the proportion of genitive-accusatives continues to grow slightly, to about 9.5% of singular direct objects, as against about 4% for the first scribe and 8.5% for Lavrentij's part of the Primary Chronicle. (Prepositional objects are excluded from these calculations, because the genitive-accusative is restricted to direct-object position in the Primary Chronicle and the early part of the Suzdal Chronicle. The figures given here therefore differ slightly from those in Table 2-1, where prepositional objects are included for all texts, to permit direct comparison among them.) The general pattern is thus one of gradual increase in frequency of accusative *ego* from the beginning of the manuscript to about 1170, with no clear break either where the first scribe's work ends or at the end of the Primary Chronicle.[7] The increase is apparently more gradual than in the Synod Manuscript, but, on the other hand, since the numbers are larger, incrementation can be slower. The usage of the Laurentian Chronicle up to about 1170 is more conservative than that of the Synod Manuscript's second scribe, but less conservative than that of the first scribe.

Although the first part of the Suzdal Chronicle is not much different from the Primary Chronicle with respect to the anaphoric genitive-accusative, the Suzdal Chronicle itself shows clear internal divisions into three parts: up to about 1160 or 1170 (the boundary is unclear), from 1160 or so to about 1206, and from 1206 to the end. In order to describe the distribution of *ego* independently of any assumptions about the location of seams in the text, I divided the Suzdal Chronicle's 238 masculine singular, 10 dual, and 82 plural anaphoric direct-object accusatives each into 3 equal groups. The second group of both singular and plural forms includes a disproportion of genitive-accusatives — over half of the singular genitive-accusatives in the chronicle, and a slightly higher proportion (about 65%) of the plurals. In the middle group of plural forms, 70% are genitive-accusatives, against 23% and 15% in the other groups. (See Tables 2–2 and 2–3. The figures given here do not correspond precisely to Table 2–1, because Table 2–1 includes prepositional objects and subdivides the Suzdal Chronicle uniformly across both singular and plural numbers.) In the singular, the disproportion is less striking: the middle group is 29% genitive-accusative, as against 10% and 18%. Altogether about 38% of the forms of the second groups are genitive-accusatives. The distribution is in general similar to that in the text copied by the third scribe of the Synod Manuscript. Of course, the extent of the similarity is accidental; however, the fact that such a range of statistical distribution of the genitive-accusative is found in the work of a single scribe speaks convincingly against using such variation to distinguish one chronicle scribe from another, much less for putting them in different centuries, as suggested by Dietze.

Table 2–2

Masculine singular genitive-accusative *ego* in the Suzdal Chronicle: number of occurrences of *ego* (direct-object form only) per each successive group of accusative anaphoric pronoun forms (20 groups of 11 or 12 forms each).

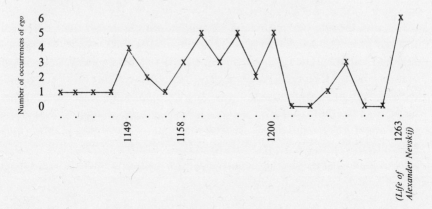

Table 2–3

Plural genitive-accusative *ix* in the Suzdal Chronicle: number of occurrences of direct object *ix* per each successive group of direct-object anaphoric accusative plural pronoun forms (20 groups of 4 or 5 forms each).*

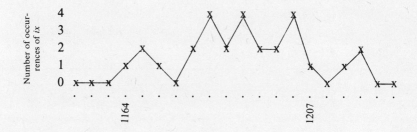

*Groups 2 and 19 have 5 elements each.

If we attempt to pinpoint the highest frequency areas more precisely within the middle part of the Suzdal Chronicle, we find that the onset of the increase is hard to locate; it is certainly no earlier than the middle of the 1150's, and is clearly in evidence by the 1160's. The maximal frequency of *ego* (calculated by subdividing the groups of forms into smaller units of equal size) is s.a. 1175 (the narrative of the death of Andrej Bogoljubskij), where we find the only occurrence of the prepositional object *nego*. The highest concentration of plurals is later, centered around approximately 1186 (the story of Igor Svjatoslavič's raid). The accusative prepositional object *nix* occurs 3 times in the narrative from 1176 to 1186. The end of the high-frequency section, unlike the beginning, is clear: after 1197 (singular) and 1207 (plural), *ego* and *ix* disappear until 1229 and 1223 respectively.

The middle portion of the Suzdal Chronicle is different from the other parts not only on the level under discussion here, but also on the level of discourse structure and thematic organization. In fact, the high-frequency segment we have isolated corresponds fairly precisely to Šaxmatov's division of the chronicle according to its putative sources. The subtleties of Šaxmatov's (1938/ 1968) and Priselkov's work on the sources of the Laurentian Manuscript are not important here; most interesting for us is the fact that Šaxmatov posited the existence of an underlying southern source containing the Primary Chronicle and the earlier part of the Suzdal Chronicle, which the compiler gradually replaced with another source, of northern origin. Basing his conclusion mainly on the geographic focus of the narrative, Šaxmatov proposed that the northern source began to be used at the very beginning of the Suzdal Chronicle, became the major source at about 1157, and completely replaced the southern source at about 1175. This northern source breaks off abruptly in 1206, when a new source, with a special interest in Rostov takes over; in 1206, also, comes the end of the Radziwill Manuscript, which follows the Laurentian closely up to that point.

The frequency curve of genitive-accusatives thus corresponds to the geographic focus of the narrative, a factor unlikely to have influenced the scribe's usage directly. The correlation between geographic setting and choice of forms is therefore to be attributed to the divergent usage of different scribes whose work eventually was included in the chronicle as we have it. The importance of source texts, and the relative unimportance of our final scribes' usage, is suggested also by the fact that the frequency of *ego*, outside of the middle part of the Suzdal Chronicle, rises very gradually and steadily across time. Thus, the distribution of the anaphoric genitive-accusative illustrates the general point that analysis of sources for chronicle texts can usefully incorporate low-level linguistic information, which can, if amassed in sufficient quantity and with respect to enough variables, provide a way of testing hypotheses originally formulated for other reasons (see Worth 1963/1977).[8] Second, the chronicles' use of source texts has to be taken into account in descriptions of their linguistic style. The stylistic range of extant texts is obviously reduced insofar as they can be viewed as overlaid and overlapping collections of source materials; each component segment of text must in principle have a narrower stylistic range than the chronicle manuscript as a whole, and more characteristics have to be treated as individual rather than with respect to a large class of occurrences from which a norm can emerge. The fact that an exhaustive segmentation of manuscripts according to their sources is not in most cases practicable does not alter the general likelihood that conscious style in the chronicles may, more often than we can find out, be very much more a readers' creation than the creation of authors.

Accusative *ego* (although usually not *ix*) is of some interest in this connection, because in some, but not all, of the sections into which we have divided the manuscripts, *ego* apparently functions as a Slavonic element, either as a conscious element of style or, more probably, as a quotation form taken out of Slavonic sources (see §2.3.1.2 and Klenin 1983). The usage in the middle section of the Suzdal Chronicle and in, roughly, the last scribe's section of the Novgorod Chronicle does not apparently distinguish Slavonic and non-Slavonic norms for *ego* or *ix*, and uses both forms more frequently than the rest of the chronicle texts. It is not clear whether the two sections with frequent and apparently unrestricted *ego* and *ix* represent just an extension of the more restricted usage. It is likely that the extension of *ix* was motivated by non-Slavonic factors, and was relatively independent of Slavonic usage.[9] In any event, it is clear that stating conditions of occurrence valid for part but not all of a manuscript assumes that the manuscript can be legitimately segmented into the parts required by the analysis; we have seen above that such segmentation depends not only on the scribal habits of the final copyists but also on those of their predecessors. Since the basis for a correct textual segmentation can never be clear a priori, it is important to rely whenever possible on groupings inherent in the data themselves, as shown above.

3.2 *Restrictions on accusative ego and ix in the chronicle texts.*

As described in the preceding subsection, the 14th-century chronicle texts fall into several large sections, according to the scribes who copied them and their sources. Not all these sections are well defined, but they are in principle firmly established and for convenience will be referred to in the following discussion as though their boundaries were clear. With respect to the distribution of the anaphoric genitive-accusative, the sections all fit one of three patterns:

A. Narrowly restricted use of *ego,* and *ix* is rare or nonoccurrent.
B. Fairly widespread use of both *ego* and *ix*, but both forms are syntactically restricted.
C. Very common use of both *ego* and *ix*, but *ix* is proportionately more frequent than *ego* and is the commonest anaphoric plural accusative form.

The Novgorod Chronicle's first, second, and third scribes produced sections corresponding, respectively, to the first, second, and third categories listed above. As noted above, the division of the Synod Manuscript according to the scribes who worked on it is artificial, and the section copied by the second scribe has clear internal divisions. Since, however, the three hands provide convenient and generally accepted boundaries, we will continue to refer to them, making occasional adjustments as needed. As noted in the preceding section, the Laurentian Manuscript's internal divisions do not correspond to different hands in the manuscript. The Primary and early Suzdal Chronicles fit category A above, the last (13th-century) part of the narrative belongs to category B, and the middle part belongs to category C (see Table 2–1).

In texts in categories A and B, accusative *ego* and *ix* are restricted nearly entirely to environments that are syntactically complex. For example, the anaphoric accusative object of a present active participle, or of a participle in a dative absolute construction, is always genitive-accusative, even in texts where the anaphoric genitive-accusative is otherwise rare.[10] Moreover, the very few examples of accusative *ego* that occur in these sections and that are objects of personal verb forms are all in passages with religious themes. This combination of syntactic and thematic restrictions indicates that *ego* was mainly a Slavonic element, either taken from religious source texts or an element of Slavonic style. It does not represent a colloquial innovation in these passages, although it may do so elsewhere in the same manuscript or chronicle.

3.2.1 Conditions on *ego* in the work of the first two scribes of the Synod Manuscript. The distribution of *ego* and *ix* in the Synod Manuscript has been studied by Istrina (1923:154–155), who notes the following two occurrences of accusative *ego* in the work of the first scribe (there are no examples of *ix*):

(30) *ide arxep(isko)pъ novъgorodьskyi nifontъ vъ rou/s/. pozvanъ izęslavomь i klimomь mitropolitomь. stavilъ bo jego bęše izęsla/v/ sъ jep(isko)py rus/s/kyja oblasti. ne slavъ c(esa)rjugra/d/(u)*
      'Nifont, Archbishop of Novgorod, went to Rus', called by Izjaslav and the Metropolitan Klim; for Izjaslav had appointed him with the bishops of the Rusian region, without sending to Constantinople' (leaf 25v, line 16 – leaf 26, 3)

(31) *a samogo s(vja)toslava jaša na pouti smolnęne i strěžaxoutь jego na smędině vъ manastyri jakože i ženou jego Novegorodě ou s(vja)toje varvary vъ manastyri*
      'and the people from Smolensk seized Svjatoslav himself on the road and they guarded him on the Smjadina in a monastery, and his wife likewise in Novgorod in a monastery at St. Barbara's' (leaf 20, line 2ff.)

The second example should probably be excluded here, however, because the verb *strěžaxut'* can govern the genitive case, as is illustrated by the following passages cited from Sreznevskij (3[1903]:573):

(32) *ö/t/ někyixъ stregouščixъ domou svojego*
      'by some guarding their houses' (*Nest. Žit. Feod.* 24)

(33) *strežašetь oboju puti*
      'he guarded both roads' (*Lavr.* s.a. 1263/6771)

(34) *starěišina povelě slugamъ svoimъ na městě tomъ strešči s(vja)togo těla.*
      'the elder ordered his servants on that place to guard the holy body'. (*Nest. Bor. Gl.* 28)

Thus, the first example above is the only clear accusative *ego* in the first scribe's section of the Synod Manuscript.

All of the second scribe's anaphoric genitive-accusatives occur in just three portions of his text: in the tale of the capture of Constantinople, under the year 1204 (leaves 64 to 72), in the tale of the Tatar invasion under the year 1224 (leaves 95v to 99v), and in the narrative for the years 1227 to 1233 (leaves 101 to 118). The two tales in particular contain a high concentration of genitive-accusative forms (8 out of the 15 in the whole of the second scribe's work), but the numbers involved are so small that this fact could be accounted for by purely random fluctuation. What is significant, however, is the contrast between these three sections of the second scribe's text and the rest of it. Leaving aside the two tales, the narrative section 1227–1233, with its 7 genitive-accusatives out of 31 eligible anaphoric accusatives, can be directly compared with the other narrative passages copied by the same scribe, which contain 30 eligible forms but no genitive-accusatives. There is no comparable grouping in the work of the third scribe, and its presence in the second scribe's work suggests, at least preliminarily, that the genitive-accusative was restricted to certain texts or kinds of texts — that is, that the presence of *ego* is correlated with elements of discourse structure or narrative content.

3.2.1.1 The syntax of *ego* in the work of the second scribe. Can the environments for accusative *ego* and *ix* be defined more narrowly, at the level of the sentence or clause, for example? There are rough syntactic correlates of the appearance of accusative *ego/ix*, but none that can be well defined. Most obviously, the second scribe's genitive-accusatives are all direct objects, and not objects of prepositions, but there are throughout his text only five prepositional phrases in which the genitive-accusative pronoun could have appeared. Other syntactic conditions are even more elusive. Of the seven anaphoric genitive-accusatives in the 1227–1233 section, two are direct objects of participles:

(35)   *ougonivše ixъ*
       'having caught up with them' (109v, 16)

(36)   *bivъše jego okovaša i*
       'having beaten him they bound him' (115v, 4–5)

and one is modified by an active participle:

(37)   *oustrětoša ixъ begajušče*
       'they met them fleeing' (103v, 16–17)

A fourth example is an object of an imperative:

(38)   *pokoi jego sъ vsemi pravъdъnymi*
       'give him rest with all the just' (117, 5–6)

and a fifth example is in a subordinate clause embedded below an active participle:

(39)   *tъgda /ž/(e) okanъnyi dijavolъ ispъrva ne xotęi dobra rodou čl(o)v(ě)čju i zaviděvъ jemou zane progonęšetъ jego. noščnutъ stojaniemъ pěnijemъ i m(o)l(i)tvami. i vъzdviže na arsenija mou/ž/(a) krotka i smerena kramolou veliku prostouju čędъ*

'And then the accursed devil, from the first not wishing the human race well and envying him because he had chased him off with nocturnal vigil, singing, and prayers, and he raised up against Arsenij, a meek and mild man, a great rebellion, the simple people' (106, 4 ff.)

The other two examples are direct objects of finite personal verb forms in simple sentences (see below).

In this same section of text, there are 24 anaphoric accusatives that could have occurred as genitive-accusatives but did not. Two are objects of prepositions; the rest are direct objects of finite personal verb forms. In this section, then, there is a very heavy concentration of genitive-accusative forms in environments of some syntactic complexity; however, the genitive-accusative also occurs in environments that are not complex at all (as shown below), and there is no single syntactic phenomenon that can be identified as a unique trigger for the genitive-accusative.

In the rest of the narrative copied by the second scribe, we find 30 forms that could have occurred as anaphoric genitive-accusatives, but none that actually did. We do find two anaphoric direct objects of active participles:

(40)   *izmavъ ja vsę posla iskovavъ*
       'having seized them all he sent them, having bound (them)' (83, 1 ff.)
(41)   *novgorodci že ougonivъše i jaša. i vedoša i na gorodišče.*
       'but the Novgorodians, having caught up to him, seized him and led him to the Gorodišče' (90, 13–14)

This shows that active participles do not always condition the genitive-accusative. Of the other 28 anaphoric accusatives, one is the object of a preposition, and the others are direct objects of personal finite verbs in simple sentences. Thus, we continue to find a pattern in which the genitive-accusative is concentrated unusually heavily in syntactically complex environments, but such environments do not guarantee the appearance of the genitive-accusative, and the genitive-accusative can also occur elsewhere.

If we broaden our data base to include the tales and the work of the third scribe, we are confronted with texts in which the genitive-accusative is nearly as common as the nongenitive accusative, and we would expect the restrictions on the genitive-accusative to be relaxed. Here it is helpful to look not just at the conditions in which the genitive-accusative appears, but also at the environments where we find the nongenitive forms. In the work of the third scribe, the nongenitive accusative occurs 48 times, once as the direct object of an active participle:

(42)   *deržavъ novgorodcevъ i novotoržcevъ ... ï odarivъ ja*
       "having detained the Novgorodians and Novotoržokians and having given them gifts' (120, 14–16)

Elsewhere, it occurs only as the object either of prepositions or of personal verb forms. The genitive-accusative, on the other hand, occurs in both of these environments, as well as in others. It occurs, for example, as the object of an infinitive:

(43) *xotěša ixъ isěšči*
'they wanted to cut them down' (142, 5–6)

In the two tales, there are similar examples:

(44) *pou(sti)ti ixъ*
'to release them' (99, 7)
(45) *posadęče jego*
'seating him' (65v, 13)
(46) *biite ixъ ö/t/tolě*
'fight them from there' (97v, 11)

The tales have no examples of nongenitive anaphoric accusatives as objects of nonpersonal verb forms. Thus, even in parts of the manuscript with very heavy use (over 40%) of genitive-accusative forms, there is a tendency to use the genitive-accusative disproportionately often in environments other than the most basic types of simple sentences with personal finite verb forms. It is impossible, however, to derive from the syntactic correlation just described anything like a syntactic explanation for the occurrence of the genitive-accusative. Not only have we left vague our definition of syntactic complexity, but, in addition, we find the genitive-accusative in environments of no apparent complexity at all. Two examples from the work of the second scribe are relevant here, and they are given below:

(47) *togo /ž(e)/ lě/t/(a) ižgoša vъlxvy 4 tvoręxutь je potvory dějušče a b(og)ъ věstь i sъžgoša ixъ na jarosla(v)li dvore*
'The same year they burned 4 wizards, they said they cast spells, but God knows, and they burned them in Jaroslav's Yard'. (102v, 19 ff.)
(48) *vъ to /ž(e)/ lěto kn(jaz)ь mixailь stvori postrěgy s(y)n(o)vi svojemou rostisl-a/v/(u) novegorodě ou sv(ja)těi sofii i ouja vla/s/ arxep(isko)pъ spiridon i posadi jego na stolě a samь poide vъ cьrnigovъ*
'The same year Prince Michael tonsured his son Rostislav at Novgorod in St. Sofia, and Archbishop Spiridon removed his hair. And he anointed him and himself went to Černigov'. (110, 18 ff.)

The sole anaphoric genitive-accusative used by the first scribe — example (30) above — also lacks any clear syntactic conditioning, as do 5 of the 8 examples in the two tales. For this reason, in spite of the correlation between the use of the genitive-accusative and its government by nonpersonal or nonfinite verb forms, this correlation by itself does not fully characterize the distribution of the genitive-accusative in the Synod Manuscript. In those parts of the manuscripts where the use of *ego/ix* is relatively infrequent (roughly, the work of the first two scribes), there is no evidence of particularly strong syntactic constraints on the genitive-accusative; thus, there is no evidence of generalization out of particular syntactic environments into a broader range of usage. Instead, the work of the first two scribes suggests that *ego*, for them, was restricted to just certain kinds of texts, which are characterized inter alia by a propensity toward syntactic complexity. This syntactic complexity, moreover, was particularly likely to favor the use of the anaphoric genitive-accusative. Consequently, in the work of the first two scribes, our description has to refer to the syntactic factors mentioned above, but relies ultimately on discourse-level information: variation in usage among different types of source texts (such as church documents, as distinct from secular sources) and thematically conditioned variation within a single text. Thus, the statistical clumping of accusative *ego* in the earlier parts of the manuscript reflects discourse-level influences on language; in this respect, the work of the third scribe is clearly different, since no such clumping can be observed. As will be explained below, it is quite likely that the expansion of the plural *ix*, which is very frequent in the parts of the chronicle texts categorized as Type C above, was motivated partly by factors not in evidence in the earlier parts of these same manuscripts. For this reason, the different parts of the chronicle manuscripts should be analyzed somewhat differently with respect to the anaphoric genitive-accusative, even independently of the increased frequency of *ego* in the Type C passages.

3.2.1.2 The status of *ego* as a Slavonicism. In characterizing the distribution of *ego* in the Type A and Type B parts of the Synod Manuscript, we noted that syntactic conditions on *ego* are not well defined. At the same time, it is clear that, in these passages, *ego* is restricted to certain kinds of writing, or writing drawn from certain sources (characterized by religious function or geographic origin), and tends to occur together with certain types of syntactic complexity. In the absence of any clear syntactic conditioning, *ego* generally appears (in these parts of the chronicle texts) in passages either with religious subject matter or, in the case of the two tales in the Novgorod Chronicle, with some literary pretensions. This combination of factors is, of course, characteristic of what is conventionally called Slavonic writing, and, for this reason, it seems fair to conclude that, in the parts of the chronicle manuscripts where its occurrence is fairly closely restricted, *ego* is characteristically Slavonic, and represents a literary or at least quasi-literary influence, rather than a colloquial innovation. There is no evidence that the status of *ego* was uniform throughout either of the two manuscripts under consideration; therefore, the Slavonic status of *ego* cannot have been particularly vivid for the 14th-century scribes, who seem to have done rather little to impose their own stamp on their texts in this respect. Hence, we may say, not that *ego* was a Slavonic element in our manuscripts, but rather that it must have been a Slavonic element for some authors of some of our manuscripts' sources.

However, in pushing back the level at which the distinction between Slavonic and non-Slavonic writing is said to be relevant, we are necessarily weakening the stylistic value of the distinction — not only for our extant text, but also for the source texts. To some extent, we may say that the distinction is weakened exactly insofar as our extant texts are true compilations (or copies of compilations), rather than simple copies of single sources. As noted above (§3.1.2), if the compiler of the extant text drew on several different kinds of sources, then the sources that chronicle religious events and discuss religious subjects may well have been written in a language indistinguishable from the language of the liturgical texts discussed in section 2 above, where the use of *ego* was fairly widespread. While it cannot at the time have been colloquial in native East Slavic, the appearance of *ego* was motivated in the ways already discussed (§2); it was probably conditioned syntactically, and was not an element of conscious stylistic choice. On the other hand, *ego* simply did not occur in other, presumably secular and more colloquial, sources. Thus, the use of *ego* need have had no particular stylistic value in the sources from which the chronicles were compiled, and, if the compilation simply represents the usage of its sources, then it had no stylistic value for the chronicle's original compiler. We have already spoken of the difficulty in ascribing stylistic intent to the scribes of our extant manuscripts. Therefore, there is no stage in the creation of our extant chronicle manuscripts at which we can reasonably imagine some individual writer consciously *selecting* the genitive-accusative because of its appropriateness in a particular passage — in spite of the fact that, in our chronicle texts, the use of the genitive-accusative is actually so restricted, and can be perceived as stylistically conditioned by later readers.

Even if, however, we restrict our attention to the extant chronicle manuscripts, it must be kept in mind that the notion of a Slavonic (or non-Slavonic) environment is not well defined. Although much of what has been said above has depended on distinguishing certain large text fragments from one another, we have deliberately avoided referring to any fine divisions of the text into narrative episodes. The reason for this is that, with the exception of certain crude divisions such as the tales already mentioned, there is in general little basis for dividing the text into discrete passages. As a result, the notion of a Slavonic environment (usually defined in terms of religious or secular subject matter, or on the basis of the linguistic "key" of a well-defined passage) is considerably weakened.[11]

The problem of thematic segmentation can be illustrated using the distribution of *iže* in the Novgorod Chronicle (Synod Manuscript). The pronoun *iže* is one of several relativizers in the manuscript, and it is generally considered a Slavonicism, conditioned by religious subject matter. However, it can occur in the same sentence with non-Slavonic pleophonic forms, such as *gorod* or *golova* instead of *grad* or *glava*, for example:

(49) *a pokoï g(ospod)i vъ c(a)r/s/tviï svoe/m/ d(u)ša těxъ iže ou goroda t(o)/g/o golovy svoja položiša za s(vja)touju sofьju*
'and the Lord give rest in his kingdom to the souls of those who at that town laid down their heads for St. Sofia'. (153v, 3–5)

Presumably, *iže* is conditioned by the religious content of the sentence, whereas *goroda* and *golovy* are conditioned by the larger context, a battle narrative, to which (49) above serves as the concluding piety following an otherwise secular description. At the same time, however, the word *gorod* also appears in the nonpleophonic form, which can occur without any specifically Slavonic context. Thus, immediately following (49) above, we go on to read:

(50) *v lě/t/(o) 6810 založiša goro/d/ kamenъ novougorodou. t(o)/g/o že lě/t/(a) založiša c(e)rk(o)vъ kamenou s(vja)toju borisa ï glěba. kotoraja porjušila sę*
'In the year 1302, they laid stone ramparts for Novgorod. The same year they built a stone church dedicated to SS. Boris and Gleb, which had fallen down'. (153v, 6–10)

Here, we find the non-Slavonic relativizer *kotoraja* instead of *iže*. Because of the presence of *kotoraja*, we might wish to view the sentence in which it occurs as secular — a narrative that happens to be about a church. In that case, however, what can we say about the following case:

(51) *t(o)/g/o že lě/t/(a) s(vja)šč(e)na by(stь) c(e)rky kamenaja s(vja)t(o)go nikoly. v nerevьskomь konci. juže sozda arxiep(isko)pъ d(a)v(y)dъ. ï stvori v nei vsed(e)nьnouju sloužbu ï černьci sovъkoupi*
'The same year there was dedicated the stone church of St. Nicholas in the Nerevskij district, which Archbishop David founded and he held daily services in it and gathered monks'. (158, 5–9)

The crucial difference between (50) and (51) may well be that consecrating churches is a religious act and having them fall down is not; if valid, however, the distinction does not lend itself to easy generalization, and it is precisely the general nature of the problem that is at issue. The few examples given here illustrate the widespread difficulties in characterizing Slavonic environments — either because it is unclear whether the relevant environment is the whole narrative episode or only some more immediate context, or else because it is actually unclear whether the content of a given passage is religious or secular.

In addition to the uncertainties involved in delimiting text segments, the notion of Slavonicisms in the chronicles is also complicated by its heterogeneity. Besides thematic considerations, Slavonic environments are usually also defined by the presence of linguistic Slavonicisms, for example, present active participles in *šč*, dative absolute constructions, or relative clauses introduced by *iže*. As is well known, the precise inventory of Slavonicisms, the extent to which they are specific to Slavonic texts, and their relation to non-Slavonic equivalents are all points open to debate. However, roughly speaking, *iže* in the Synod Manuscript can fairly be called a Slavonicism because of its tendency to occur in religious passages and because it competes with other relative pronouns that are clearly not Slavonic. Similarly, *begajušče* in (37) above is Slavonic, in that no participle need have been used at all, and, if one were used, the equivalent form in *č* was also, at least theoretically, possible. Linguistic Slavonicisms often occur together, and multiple Slavonicisms typically occur in religious narrative, as can be seen from the examples above. However, classification of an environment as Slavonic can in principle be based on either of two independent criteria, and thematic criteria, without any accompanying linguistic correlates, are crucial in classifying as Slavonic the passage given as (30) above. In the work of the first two scribes of the Synod Manuscript, occurrence of *ego* is thus highly correlated with Slavonic environments, but the notion of a Slavonic environment has to be understood to be itself a complex of factors whose interrelations are not entirely established.

Finally, with respect to the Slavonic character of the environments of *ego* in the work of the first two scribes of the Synod Manuscript, it may be noted that there are two examples of *ego* as the direct object of a past active participle — (35) and (36) above. As noted, the past active participle also occurs with nongenitive accusative anaphoric objects in the work of the second and third scribes, even in parts of the text where the genitive-accusative is generally widespread in all kinds of constructions. The past active participle is not itself particularly Slavonic, although of course it is not excluded from Slavonic, and it seems to be a marginal category for conditioning the genitive-accusative. It is possible that the past active participles began to take the genitive-accusative only because of their general status as subordinative elements, and because, if the present active participles (which are Slavonic by form) conditioned the genitive-accusative, then the past active participle would tend to do so also.

To conclude our discussion of the Novgorod Chronicle, we may note that the use of *ego* in its earlier sections seems to have been conditioned by Slavonic contexts, probably representing the usage in original Slavonic source texts. However, the notion of a Slavonic context is not well defined, and involves the interaction of syntactic factors with thematic ones. It is not very likely that the choice of genitive or nongenitive form was directly conditioned by stylistic choice on the part of the scribes of our extant manuscript. Although the conditions on the occurrence of *ego* have only been rather weakly defined, nevertheless it has been shown that the strongest environments favoring the genitive-accusative in the Novgorod Chronicle were not apparently collo-quial, but were, on the contrary, associated with a certain degree of complexity and literariness.

3.2.2 Conditions on the anaphoric genitive-accusative in the Laurentian Manuscript of 1377.

3.2.2.1 The Primary Chronicle.
I have described elsewhere (Klenin 1980c, Klenin 1983) the syntactic conditions in which accusative *ego* and *ix* appear in the Primary Chronicle. In this text, the anaphoric genitive-accusative is less frequent than in the work of either the second or the third Novgorod scribe — about 6.0% of about 354 possible occurrences. The genitive-accusative occurs only in direct-object position, and is mainly restricted to the singular. Thus, the Primary Chronicle is more conservative, in these respects also, than either the second or third Novgorod scribes. Most genitive-accusatives occur in environments that can be characterized as syntactically relatively complex, for example, in participial phrases, such as the following:

(52) *kr(e)/s/tъ bo vskorě izbavlęe/t/ ö/t/ napastii prizyvajušči/m/ jego s věroju*
'for the cross quickly saves from snares for those–calling on it with faith'
(58b 24–26)

Here, the genitive-accusative is the direct object of the participle *prizyva-juščim*. Singular anaphoric direct objects of long-form participles occur only in the genitive-accusative (a total of four occurrences). Only the genitive-accusative occurs as the direct object of a dative absolute, in either singular or plural, for example:

(53) *m(a)t(e)ri bo rodivši jego by(stъ) jemu jazveno na glavě jego*
'for when his mother bore him, there was a caul on his head' (52c 21–23)

(54) *i ne öčjutiša ixъ polovci b(og)u sxranšju ixъ*
'and the Polovcians did not detect them, God saving them' (77a 9–10)

There are also environments in which the genitive-accusative occurs, but the nongenitive accusative is also found; one such environment is the past active participle, for example:

(55) *ön že ... postriže i ... nakazavъ jego*
'and he ... tonsured him ... and instructed him' (53a 10–12)

(56)   *poxvalite ego vsi lju/d/(i)e*
       'praise him all the people' (33b27)

And, finally, there is one example that has no obvious syntactic explanation:

(57)   *i r(eč)e jemu jako ö/t/ tebe mnozi černьсï byti imutь bl(a)g(oslo)vi i i ö/t/pusti*
       jego rekъ jemu idi s miromь
       'And he said to him "from you many monks will come" and blessed him and
       released him saying to him "go in peace".' (53a 15ff.)

The breakdown is remarkably similar even in detail to that in the Novgorod
Chronicle, in the work of the first two scribes. Most occurrences of accusative
ego and *ix* can be described in terms of one or another type of syntactic
complexity. The past active participle is a less good environment than the
present active participle, and there is an example with no clear syntactic
trigger for *ego*, where, however, the content of the passage is religious. As in
the Synod Manuscript, most of the syntactically conditioned examples are
also religious in theme. (The remaining examples, not given above, appear in
Klenin 1980c). It may be noted that the anaphoric accusative in the Primary
Chronicle is in general very infrequent in liturgical and other religious contexts, as compared with its frequency in secular narrative; for this reason, the
concentration of genitive-accusatives in religious environments is all the more
striking.

3.2.2.2 The Suzdal Chronicle.

The pattern of distribution of *ego* in the
Suzdal Chronicle has already been partly described above. The first and last
parts of the Suzdal Chronicle show roughly the same distribution as the
Primary Chronicle, although with gradually increasing frequency of *ego*.
Thus, even the 13th-century parts of the narrative still have *ego* primarily as a
Slavonic element, in contrast not only to the middle part (ca. 1170–1206) of
the same chronicle but also to the later parts of the Synod Manuscript of the
Novgorod Chronicle (from 1234). This suggests dialectal variation in the
status of *ego* in the East Slavic area in the late 12th and 13th century. The usage
of these more conservative parts of the Suzdal Chronicle is illustrated in the
following examples:

(58)   *postavi kivotъ v s(vę)těi b(ogorodi)cě ... i oukrasi jego*
       'he placed a reliquary in the Church of the Holy Mother of God ... and
       painted it' (s.a. 1237, leaf 159v)
(59)   *i ljude/m/ s mitropolito/m/ srětši/m/ jego. i posadiša i na stolě praděda svojego*
       Jaroslava.
       'and the people and the metropolitan meeting him, and they seated him on
       the throne of his great-grandfather Jaroslav'. (s.a. 1138, leaf 102)
(60)   *i položi jego ... položiša i*
       'and he placed him ... they placed him' (s.a. 1237, leaf 163)

(61) *bl(a)g(slo)vi jego i ö/t/pusti*
'blessed him and dismissed him' (s.a. 1263, leaf 168v – Life of Alexander Nevskij)

The middle part of the chronicle, as noted above, makes extensive use not only of *ego* but also of *ix*. Although these genitive-accusatives still are particularly likely to appear as objects of participles, they are so frequent as to be virtually unrestricted. Whatever vestigial conditions remain on the occurrence of the genitive-accusative, they are syntactic, and are apparently unrelated to narrative content or to Slavonic influence as such. Examples from the middle part of the Suzdal Chronicle include the following ones:

(62) *za grěxy navede na ni/x/*
'for their sins (God) brought (it) upon them'. (leaf 129v, s.a. 1177)
(63) *ěxavš/e/ v voronožь jaša jego sami. i privedoša jego v volodimerъ. i vsadiša i tu že*
'going to Voronež they seized him themselves and brought him to Volodimer' and imprisoned him there'. (s.a. 1177, leaf 130v)
(64) *polovci že ouslyšavše rusь öže prišli na ni/x/.*
'but when the Polovcians heard that the Rus' had come (to fight) against them' (s.a. 1185, leaf 133v)

The very high frequency of the plural genitive-accusative requires special comment. As noted, texts using *ego* as a Slavonic element use accusative *ix* rarely if at all. In the other sections of the Laurentian Manuscript, the only regular accusative plural form is *ja*, itself an originally Slavonic form. The East Slavic equivalent *ě* (generally spelled *e*) is rare in the Laurentian Manuscript, although it is the regular form in the work of the second Novgorod scribe, even in the two tales and other apparently Slavonic contexts. In the early and middle parts of the Suzdal Chronicle, however, there are about 15 occurrences of the form *i* as an accusative plural (including 2 occurrences of *nъ* for expected *nę*). The following examples are typical:

(65) *smirivъ že sę s Polovci i podarivъ i*
'having made peace with the Polovcians and given them gifts' (leaf 120v, s.a. 1169)
(66) *i srětoša i paki i sstupišasę s nimi bitъ*
'and they met them again and started to fight with them' (leaf 122v, s.a. 1171)
(67) *a se vorozi tvoi i naši ... ljubo i kazni ljubo slěpi ali dai na/m/*
'but these are your enemies and ours ... either execute them or blind them or give them to us' (leaf 130v, s.a. 1177)

In these and a few similar passages, the Radziwill Manuscript replaces *i* with the expected *ja*. The use of *i* here is presumably an example of slightly puzzling nominative-accusative syncretism — puzzling, since the hypothetical nominative does not in fact occur, although the nominative plural *iže* naturally is well attested. This form was multiply ambiguous, moreover, since it was the regular masculine singular accusative. To the extent that nominative-accusative syncretism was an important factor in the rise of the anaphoric genitive-accusative (and, as suggested in §2, its importance in the growth of accusative *ego* was probably considerable), then the appearance of an accusative plural *i* probably helped advance the spread of accusative *ix*. In any event, the competition among several different accusative forms probably in itself would have tended to make easier the spread of the already marginally possible genitive-accusative plural.

3.3 Conclusions.

It can be concluded from the discussion above that the Primary Chronicle, the beginning and end of the Suzdal Chronicle, and the first two thirds of the Novgorod Chronicle (Synod Manuscript) all use the anaphoric genitive-accusative in Slavonic environments, although with increasing frequency across time. The Slavonic use of the genitive-accusative is partly conditioned by syntax, and there is some evidence of syntactic conditioning on the genitive-accusative even in the other parts of the chronicle texts, where, however, *ego* and *ix* are so common as to be considered the normal form. The usage in these other parts of the chronicles probably ought not to be viewed as simply an expansion from the usage in the more conservative sections, however, especially in view of the special problem of competing accusative forms in the middle section of the Suzdal Chronicle. Although the personal usage of the scribes of our extant manuscripts no doubt influenced their distribution of the genitive-accusative to some extent (cf. in this respect the changes introduced by the scribe of the Radziwill Manuscript), the usage of the chronicle manuscripts for the most part probably represents that of earlier texts. This is shown by the extreme heterogeneity of our manuscripts; not only do they vary internally with respect to the frequency of occurrence of *ego* and *ix*, but they also show the influence of factors unlikely to have influenced our scribes directly — gradual increase over time, and a preference for the genitive-accusative in narrative with a northern setting. For this reason, the Slavonic status of *ego* in certain parts of the manuscripts must be understood to refer to the nature of particular sources, and not to the stylistic choices of our scribes. On the other hand, the variation in usage according to geographic setting suggests that there may have been dialectal variation in the distribution of *ego* and *ix* in the later 12th and 13th century, with the north and west displaying a tendency toward innovation. This impression is at least weakly confirmed by the evidence of 13th-century legal texts. In combination, the influence of earlier texts and apparent dialectal variation explain the otherwise obscure fact that the 14th-century chronicle texts, taken in their entirety, are statistically more conservative in their use of *ego* and *ix* than are either legal or religious texts of the 13th century. The religious texts' usage was discussed in the previous section, and the usage of the legal texts is discussed in the next one.

4. Legal texts.

The anaphoric genitive-accusative is not attested in legal documents from before 1200. In the period from 1200 to 1300, there are about 15 occurrences of accusative *ego* and *ix*, about a quarter of the 60 anaphoric masculine accusative pronouns. In the Russkaja Pravda, the proportion is only 3 out of 24 (12.5%), whereas in treaties the proportion is 12 out of 36 (33%); although the corpus is too small for this variation to be very significant in itself, it does conform to expectations formed on other grounds: the Russian Law Code is highly conservative, whereas the treaties, as will be explained below, are innovatory. The nongenitive accusative form occurs beside the genitive-accusative in all but one of our texts, but there are no 13th-century texts containing only the nongenitive form. Since there are also no religious texts containing a significant corpus that lack the genitive-accusative, and the early chronicle texts also both contain abundant examples, we can conclude that the anaphoric genitive-accusative was well attested in all kinds of East Slavic and East Slavonic writing from the 13th century on. The preponderance of religious writing from before 1200 may suggest that the genitive-accusative arose simultaneously in all kinds of writing, and the earlier restriction to religious writing is only an accident of the documentation available. This, however, is unlikely, not only because it ignores the legal writing from before 1200, but, more significantly, because it leaves unexplained the distribution of genitive-accusatives in the chronicles. Thus, the appearance of the genitive-accusative in legal texts of the 13th century probably reflects a real change in norms, and not merely the weakness of earlier documentation.

Of the 15 examples of accusative *ego* and *ix*, only one is in the plural:

(68) *ö/t/poustite ixъ procь* (sic!)
      'let them go' (Novg. 1270, Šaxmatov 1885–1886:243)

Three of the remaining examples are objects of the preposition *na*, and the rest are singular direct objects.

The anaphoric genitive-accusatives in legal texts are all in subordinate clauses, or are objects of imperative or infinitive verb forms. Although this distribution is reminiscent of the syntactic restrictions in the chronicles, it is not entirely comparable. The legal texts contain hardly any simplex indicative constructions, because of the nature of their subject matter, and the nongenitive and genitive accusative forms are distributed apparently randomly in all types of constructions.

In general, the legal texts confirm the impression created in the other kinds of writing examined above, that, although the old accusative forms remained normal during the 13th century, the genitive-accusative was well established as a competing form. There are still some conditions that clearly favor the genitive-accusative: government by a nonpersonal verb form, direct-object position, and singular number, although the available corpus of legal texts does not permit any precise statements of these apparent restrictions. On the whole, the growth of the anaphoric genitive-accusative in legal language probably ought to be dated earlier than is customarily done; for example, Borkovskij (1949:363–364), in the standard work on the subject, notes that the genitive-accusative is normal in writs and charters of the very early 14th century, but considers the norm in the 13th century to be only the old accusative. To some extent, the difference between Borkovskij's view and that expressed here is a matter of phrasing: clearly the genitive-accusative was not the dominant form in our texts, but, if there are texts in which it appears in one out of three instances, then it must be considered at least not a rarity, and the dominance of the genitive-accusative in the early 14th-century texts is less unexpected than Borkovskij finds it.

Of particular value is the fact that the genitive-accusative is attested both in the Russkaja Pravda and in treaties from Smolensk and Novgorod. None of these texts can be characterized as colloquial, but the differences among them are such that, if the genitive-accusative occurs in all of them, then it cannot have been narrowly restricted to just one or another kind of language. Moreover, because each of the texts is unique of its kind, the appearance of *ego* in just one of them would be hard to evaluate.

The Russkaja Pravda in the 1282 version being discussed here constitutes about a dozen leaves in a much longer compilation of church law. Although the language of the Russkaja Pravda is a subject of controversy (see Obnorskij 1934/1960, Seliščev 1941/1957/1968, and others), its origins as a codification of the law of Jaroslav Vladimirovič in the 11th century are sufficient to indicate the relatively archaic nature of its language. It is unclear what stage in the transmission of the code is reflected in its use of the genitive-accusative, since the 1282 manuscript is the earliest copy of it that we have. As noted above, it uses the genitive-accusative relatively rarely, and all three of its examples are singular direct objects. The three occurrences of accusative *ego* in the 1282 text are as follows:

(69)   *ože li gospodinъ ötsletь jego na svoje öroudьje*

'if the master sends him off on some errand of his own' (Grekov 1:1940:130)

(70) *ače kdě nalězětъ oudarenyi tъ svojego istъča, kto že jego oudarilъ*
'if the person who has been struck somewhere finds the person who has struck him' (Grekov 1:1940:131)

(71) *to vykoupati jego gospodinou*
'then his master has to pay his debt for him' (Grekov 1:1940:133)

(the glosses above are intended only as rough guides to the probable meanings of the extracts; they are based on the interpretations found in Grekov 2[1947], pages 489, 535, and 730 respectively.)

On the other hand, the treaties are all either originals or copies of texts that originated in the 13th century, and even represent special kinds of treaties, lacking earlier models in East Slavic writing. In this respect, the 1270 Novgorod treaty, whose sole anaphoric genitive-accusative is cited above as (68), is the most straightforward, although, grammatically, (68) is actually among the least clear of our examples. The verb is apparently a plural imperative, although the addressee was just one person, Prince Jaroslav Jaroslavič, who, according to the usage of contemporary documents, should surely have been addressed in the singular. According to Šaxmatov (1886:158, 243), the earlier edition of the treaty reads the form as *otpusti*, but he adds that the plural *-te* is perfectly clear in the original. Šaxmatov himself proposes that the final *-e* of the word is a mistake for intended *-i*, making the form an infinitive. Both the infinitive and the imperative occur in contexts quite similar to the one in question, but the phrase *otpusti ixъ proč* occurs in the 1304–1305 treaty between Novgorod and Prince Mixail Jaroslavič in the same article where the 1270 treaty has *otpustite*. The treaty's language is in other respects not particularly difficult, but it should be noted that this text is only the third of its kind in East Slavic, and the first two were nearly contemporary, from 1264 and 1266 respectively. (See Kočin 1939 for additional analysis of the language of the three treaties as a group.) All three treaties are addressed to Jaroslav, who was invited to be prince at Novgorod in January 1264, some two months after the death of his brother Alexander Nevskij. Jaroslav was dependent on the Mongols, who decided on his trade relations with Riga (see Valk #30) and supported him militarily, both against the Germans in 1269 and against his own city of Novgorod when it expelled him in 1270. The treaty in which (68) above occurs represents the end of this episode, and the approval of the document by the khanate is noted on the back (the seals have apparently been lost): "Se priexaša posly ot Mengu Temergja c(a)rja sažatъ Jaroslava sъ gramotoju Cěvgu i Baiši". There are no such treaties from the pre-Mongol period. Thus, the treaties of 1264–1270 represent a new kind of document, a Russian administrative record of the Golden Horde.

All the other 13th-century anaphoric genitive-accusatives are in trade treaties between Smolensk and the Teutonic Knights at Wisby and Riga. The forms in question are in five manuscripts, representing two such treaties, one made in 1229 and the other probably in 1223 to 1225, according to Sumnikova (1963:14–17). The 1229 treaty exists in six copies (excluding one made by Karamzin — see Sumnikova 1963:180 of which four, called A, B, D, and E, are from the 13th century, and are therefore included here. The four copies of the 1229 treaty represent two different redactions — the so-called Gothland redaction (copies A and B) and the Riga redaction (copies D and E). Because all five manuscripts contain many parallel passages, their language can easily be compared in detail. In general, they show no real consistency in their use of anaphoric forms. For example, one of the two genitive-accusatives in the 1223–1225 treaty occurs in the following passage:

(72) *aže netьčicь koupitь vъ rizě ... ou smolnęnina tovarъ. ponesetь ego domovь. a vъsxočetь vorotiti. smolnęninou že tъtъ tъvarъ ne nadobe bole*
'if a German buys in Riga ... merchandise of a Smolensker, takes it home. but decides to return (it), then the Smolensker need not (take) that merchandise anymore'. (§17, lines 52–55; Avanesov 1963:12)

All the manuscripts of the 1229 treaty contain a parallel passage, but in each instance the anaphoric *ego* is either deleted or replaced with a repetition of *tovarъ*. Similarly, Manuscript D of the 1229 treaty twice has the phrase 'one can put him in irons'; at line 37, 'him' is *i*, but at line 39, we fine *ego* — and Manuscript E in the same passages exactly reverses the two pronoun forms. Thus, the distribution of *ego* seems to be random.

As with the 1270 treaty from Novgorod, it is difficult to generalize out of the usage of the Smolensk treaties, because they are the first texts of their kind and are in some ways unique. There may have been German or Latin versions of these treaties, since German versions of similar treaties with Novgorod exist and the language of the Wisby redaction of the 1229 treaty shows clear German influence. The fact that there exist six copies of the 1229 treaty in Russian and none in any other language is not strong evidence against German or Latin versions having existed, since they might have been kept at Wisby and destroyed in the sack of Wisby in 1362. Even if our extant texts of the 1229 treaty are not translations, their language is in any event so peculiar that Kiparsky (1939, 1960) has even suggested that the original Russian text (Manuscript A in the Wisby redaction) was actually written by a native speaker of German instead of a Slav. If Kiparsky is right, of course, then the distribution of *ego* in the treaty is on the whole uninformative; in general, although Kiparsky's hypothesis cannot be proved, the evidence for it is actually strong.

The treaty was written, according to the words of the text itself, by someone called Tumaše — not a Russian name; he traveled to the German centers of Riga and Wisby on behalf of the Prince of Smolensk to treat with the Germans. At this very early stage of the trade with the Germans, it is extremely dubious that the Dvina Slavs would have had time to develop their own translators, although the German traders were extraordinarily precocious at developing translators for their side (see Stieda 1885, Goetz 1916). Consequently, if the Slavs wanted someone to represent them who knew German, they would most likely have had to rely on a native speaker. Kiparsky mentions several lexical blunders in the treaty, difficult to imagine a Russian producing even under the influence of a German source; in particular, the treaty uses the term *oustoko morę* for 'Baltic Sea' (line 10), an obvious direct translation of 'Ostsee'. For the Russians, the Baltic has never been to the east, and they referred to it as the Varangian Sea. Not only would the term *oustoko morę* have been meaningless to a Russian, but the form itself totally ignores East Slavic morphology, which should have produced something like *vostočnoe* for *oustoko*. In addition, the date of the treaty, as well as other time expressions, are rendered in German style. The opening formula (paragraph 'a' in Avanesov 1963:20) is very much like the opening of contemporary German documents, as can be seen by comparing it with the opening of the 1253 charter of Frankfurt on the Oder. The two documents are cited below:

(73) *čto sę dějetě po věretьpetъ. to ö/t/ideto po věrъtьpetъ. prikazano boudě̌te dobrymъ ljudě̌mъ. a ljubo gramotoju outvě̌rdę̌tь. kako to boudě̌te vsemъ vě̌domъ. ili kto poslь živyi östaně̌tь sę.*
'what is done in [its] time passes away in its time; it is announced to the people or confirmed with a document so that it will be known to all, whoever may remain living afterwards.'

(74) *Wenn dy czyt sache ist der vorgencglicheit, alle ding sich us der czyt voraldernn und daz alder ouch vorgessenheit inbrynget, had menschliche fursichtikeit mit geczugnissen der brive gelossen czu offinbaren den nachkomeden, daz von eynem alleyne durch syner vorgenclicheit willen mit menschlichen stymen yn nicht mochte geoffinbard werden.*
'Because time involves transitoriness, all things grow old with time, and age induces oblivion as well, therefore, by documentary evidence, human precaution makes known to those who come after that which could not be made known by just one person's voice, because of its transitoriness'. (cited from Helbig-Weinrich 1968.1.242–243)

(The formulae about the passage of time appear in texts in Helbig-Weinrich beginning about 1220, are very common for about a century thereafter, and disappear after 1346. Less elaborate formulae about writing things down so that they cannot be forgotten begin earlier, in the mid-12th century.)

Similar passages in both Latin and German are numerous in texts of the period. More interesting, however, are the four passages immediately following the formulaic introduction, where the circumstances surrounding the conclusion of the treaty are narrated; this is the only section of the treaty that is not formulaic and it might for this reason be expected to follow something like the sort of narrative style found in, say, the chronicle texts. In fact, however, the narrative is actually more opaque than the opening formula, as can be shown from its final paragraph:

(75) *Na tomъ mirou až by mirъ tvьrdъ bylъ. tako bylъ knęzju ljubo. i rižanъmъ vsemъ i vsemou latineskomou jazykou. I vsemъ temъ kto to na oustoko morę xoditъ :: až by nalъzlъ pravdou. to napsati. kako to deržati rousi. sъ latineskymъ jazykomě. i latineskomou jazykou sъ rousiju. to děržati. Až byxъmъ čto tako oučinili. togo b(og)ъ ne dai. až by promъžju nami boi bylъ. a ljubo č(e)l(o)v(ě)ka oubijutъ do sm(e)rti. kako č(e)l(o)v(ě)ka to ö/t/platiti. až by mirъ ne rъzdroušenъ bylъ :: takъ platiti. kako to by öboimъ ljubo byly ::*
'at this treaty that the treaty might be firm, such was the prince's wish, and the Riga people's and all the Latins' and all those whoever goes on the East Sea. That there should be a document, thus to write, how the Rus' were to be with the Latin tribe and the Latin tribe with Rus' how to be. So if we did anything, which God grant not happen, that there should be a fight between us, or a man is killed, how the man is to be paid for so that the peace is not broken. To pay so that it should be satisfactory to all.' (Avanesov 1963:21, 9–13)

This paragraph cannot be a reliable guide to colloquial East Slavic of the 13th century; the particle *to*, for example, in *to napisati* or *to deržati* is otherwise unknown, although a possible source for it might be a German form *to* marking the infinitive (see Nissen 1884:86–88). In any event, the fact that some of the text's most striking peculiarities occur in its least formulaic part tends to support Kiparsky's view that the person writing it down knew Russian well, but only as a language acquired for specific purposes, including writing trade agreements but not including simple story telling.

The elaborate introductory formulae and the narrative are both absent from the other Smolensk trade treaty. According to Sumnikova (see Avanesov 1963: 15–17), this treaty was a draft of the 1229 treaty and was written between 1223 and 1225. The manuscript is undated, and it is unknown where it was written down or by whom. Since it is in the first-person singular, the 'speaker' being an unknown prince of Smolensk, the document was quite likely prepared at Smolensk. It had no German signatories. The language of the treaty is free from the difficulties of the treaty from 1229, although one reason for this is that most of the difficult sections of the 1229 treaty lack analogues in the earlier one. The earlier treaty uses anaphoric accusatives far more freely than the 1229 treaty, which tends to use deletion or repetition instead of pronominalization. Altogether, the 15 anaphoric accusatives in the earlier treaty constitute about 1% of its total word count, the same as in the chronicles, and about the same as in the Russkaja Pravda. The proportion in the 1229 treaty is only about .2%

From our discussion it emerges that the 13th-century legal texts using the anaphoric genitive-accusative are in some important ways problematical, and they offer only a rather small corpus; at the same time, however, they confirm the impression created in other kinds of texts, that the anaphoric genitive-accusative was widespread even if not the dominant accusative form for the masculine singular in all kinds of East Slavic writing of their time and place. Because the texts all come from either Smolensk or Novgorod, they add little to our knowledge of the dialectal distribution of the genitive-accusative. From the early 14th century on, the genitive-accusative was the predominant form for the masculine anaphoric pronoun in all kinds of legal texts, and was apparently unrestricted either syntactically or stylistically (see Borkovskij 1949: 364 for documentation).

5. *Summary and conclusions.*

The anaphoric masculine accusative pronouns are well attested in early East Slavic writing of all kinds, and nongenitive and genitive accusative forms were in competition from the time of our earliest records. However, there were apparently restrictions of several sorts on the use of the genitive-accusative. It was used at first more in the singular than the plural, and more in direct-object than in prepositional-object position. It tends very strongly to occur as the direct object of nonpersonal verb forms, including both participles and infinitives, and to some extent imperatives also. The data, particularly, of the religious writing, confirmed by the evidence of other texts, show that the genitive-accusative arose to a very great extent on the basis of reanalyzed genitive (direct) objects, which explains at least partly the early restriction of the genitive-accusative to direct-object position. There is also some evidence that the rise of the anaphoric genitive-accusative may have been promoted by nominative-accusative syncretism, a condition well known in the history of the noun genitive-accusative; in the anaphoric pronouns, traces of such influence appear in the apparent utilization of the relative pronoun *iže* as an analogical model for the anaphoric genitive-accusative, and in the development of the accusative plural *i* in certain parts of the Suzdal Chronicle, characterized by genitive-accusative syncretism in the plural. There is no clear evidence connecting the anaphoric genitive-accusative with referential animacy, or with factors apparently relevant to the personal-pronoun genitive-accusative, in particularly stress (see Chapter Three).

The genitive-accusative in the masculine singular must have been generalized by about the beginning of the 14th century, although some conservative texts, in particular the 14th-century chronicle manuscripts, show the clear influence of earlier usage. In the period before 1300, all kinds of writing show rather wide statistical variation in the frequency of the genitive-accusative. This may well reflect dialectal variation, either among scribes of our extant texts or in their sources. Although there is insufficient evidence for a definitive statement, at least some southern sources, to judge from the Suzdal Chronicle, may have been quite conservative, even in the mid- to latter 13th century. The chronicle texts in their more conservative parts show *ego* only as a Slavonicism, but in other texts *ego* occurs apparently without connection to specifically Slavonic usage. At some point, probably in the 14th century, when the genitive-accusative had been generalized everywhere in East Slavic, the old accusative *i*, as a conservative form found in liturgical texts, apparently came to be identified as a kind of neo-Slavonicism; the persistence of *i* in religious texts through the 17th century attests to such a reinterpretation, the earliest known evidence of which is probably in the later corrections made in the Izbornik of 1076.

NOTES

1. Cf., however, van Wijk (1931:203) on *ego* as a neuter in Suprasliensis 90, 7.

2. The Old Russian transliteration used for (photocopied) manuscript citations preserves the *jat'* *(ě)*, the jus malyj *(ę)*, omega *(ö)*, *ou* digraph (for textual *ou* and the ligature), *i–desjateričnoe (ï)*, and jotation of vowels *(j)*. I have nowhere distinguished *e–poluležačee* from other *e*, because the distinction is often unclear in my texts. Occasionally, *jery* is spelled with *i* rather than *ï* in my texts, but I have transliterated both spellings as *y*. Citations from nonphotographic editions or secondary sources generally follows the usage therein, including orthographic simplifications.

When working from sources indicating superscripts and abbreviations, I have indicated them. Superscripts are in slashes (/), and abbreviations are in parentheses. Superscripts within abbreviations, however, are not set off by slashes, and the titlo is omitted throughout. Any letters actually missing from my original source text appear in parentheses. Abbreviations are resolved in the interests of readability, and are not intended to represent etymological reconstructions.

I have tried to indicate locations as clearly as possible, but the variety of my source materials did not permit a uniform notation. Manuscript leaves, columns, and line numbers are generally indicated where possible, and I also note page numbers for the Izbornik of 1076, where manuscript leaves do not appear consecutively in the published edition I used. My main source for the Suzdal Chronicle was Karskij's edition, which does not indicate line numbers. I have followed Karskij's marginal annotation of leaf and side (my *v* replacing his *ob.*), and I have also noted the year under which the given passage appears in the chronicle. In the Primary Chronicle (Laurentian Manuscript), I indicate sides *a* and *b* or (when the page is written in two columns) columns *a* through *d*. The Soviet editions I used generally indicate columns by means of cyrillic letters; I have replaced their *a, b, v, g* with roman *a, b, c, d,* so as to avoid an ambiguous use of *v*. In the Synod Manuscript of the First Novgorod Chronicle, I indicate leaf number, *v(erso)* as appropriate, and line number.

3. A similar instance of correction from *ego* to *i* occurs in the Life of Nifont, according to Rystenko (1928:328); however, it is unclear to me when or by whom the correction was made.

4. Accusative *ego* is actually less frequent in the Uspenskij Sbornik than is suggested by the index to the published text; this index lists about 40 genitive forms as accusatives.

5. Another noteworthy peculiarity of *(26)* is the presence of a lexicalized negative *ne-*; in Old Church Slavonic, unlike most Old Russian, such nonsentential negation could condition genitive case marking on direct objects.

6. With verbs meaning 'ask', the object under discussion is, of course, the person asked, not the thing requested. On *poběditi*, see also Xodova 1963:63.

7. On *ego* in the Primary Chronicle, see Klenin 1983.

8. The distinction between linguistic and nonlinguistic analytic criteria is obviously artificial, because the object of analysis is itself linguistic. Šaxmatov's analysis of the sources of the Laurentian text is not so much non- or extra- linguistic as it is based on discourse characteristics — for example, references to the Perejaslavians as 'naši' ('ours'), thereby implying a Perejaslav narrator.

9. The sections of text with frequent use of accusative *ixъ* generally show considerable variety of accusative plural forms, including both *ě* and *i*, and make less use of the normal Slavonic *ja*. See discussion below, and Chapter Four, §1.

10. Cf. the discussion of the genitive-accusative participial object in §2 above. Note also that the personal pronoun *mę* occurs in the nongenitive accusative form after participles, even though the genitive-accusative was theoretically possible. Conditions on the personal pronoun genitive-accusative are discussed in the next chapter, where it is shown that they are quite different from conditions on the anaphoric genitive-accusative.

11. On defining the linguistic "key" of a passage, see Shevelov 1968. On Slavonicisms in the chronicles, see also Hüttl-Worth 1973, Hüttl-Folter 1980, Uspenskij 1976.

Chapter Three.   Other Pronouns.

1. Introduction. Demonstrative and Indefinite Pronouns.

The history of the genitive-accusative in anaphoric pronouns is well documented, as we have seen, in East Slavic writing of all kinds; other classes of pronouns are less well represented. The genitive-accusative of demonstrative pronouns (*sь, tь, onyj, ovyj*), the emphatic pronoun (*sam, samyj*) and other nonanaphoric pronouns (*inyj, drugyj*) is apparently further advanced in our early texts than is the anaphoric or personal-pronoun genitive-accusative. An exception is the quantifier *vsě* 'all', which rarely shows the genitive-accusative *vsěxъ*. Examples of all these pronouns, however, are too infrequent to permit any useful statistical analysis. Different kinds of texts offer no clear variations in usage, and the genitive-accusative of all these forms is not syntactically or otherwise constrained in any obvious way. Examples occur in singular and plural, and with personal, animal, and possibly inanimate reference, as is shown by the examples below. In example (1), the antecedent of *togo* (genitive-accusative of demonstrative *tъ*) is the inanimate noun *krestъ* 'cross'; however, this word is sporadically treated as animate (presumably because of its meaning as 'the Crucifix'), for example in the Primary Chronicle in the Laurentian Manuscript at leaf 17b, lines 30 and 31 (two examples).

(1) [*krestъ*] *jego že ang(e)li ne mogoutь zrěti ... t(o)/g/o že my vъ rou/k/(a)x dъržašče skvěrnьny ousty cěloujemъ*
'the cross that the angels cannot behold, yet the same we holding in our hand kiss with unclean lips' (Synod Ms., 111, 4–8)

(2) *inï... troupije... jadęxou a druzii koninou psinou. košky. nъ těxъ osočivъše tako tvoręxou. ovyxъ ognьmь ižgoša. a drougyxъ osěkoša. inyxъ izvěšaša. ini že тъxъ jadęxou.*
'some ... ate ... corpses and others horseflesh, the flesh of dogs, cats, but having hunted these (people?) down, they did thus with them: some they burned in a fire, others they flayed, others they hanged (?), and some people ate moss'. (Synod Ms., 113v, 3–11)

(3) *aže boudoutь ljudije iz ynoe zemlь тъxъ poslь věsti*
'if there are people from another land, these should be brought later' (Smolensk treaty (A), 1229, Avanesov 1963:24, 82–83)

(4) *da ašče xoščete za si/x/ biti sę da se my gotovi*
'but if you want to fight for these, then we are ready' (Laurentian Ms., leaf 90b, lines 9–11)

(5) *togda arximandritъ sego prizvavъ*
'then the archimandrite having called him'. (Life of Savva, page 29, 5–6)

The genitive form is the normal accusative for these pronouns, and the non-genitive occurs after the end of the 14th century only in a few set phrases.

For the interrogative *kъto*, of course, the genitive-accusative *kogo* is the only accusative form, not only in East Slavic but anywhere in Slavic.

2. The reflexive pronoun.

The accusative reflexive pronoun *sę* occurs in early East Slavic texts as the object of a preposition, as in the following examples:

(6) *i voevati počaša sami na sę*
'and they began to war among themselves' (Laurentian Ms., 7a, 14–15)

(7) *vozmutь na sę prutьe mladoe*
'they take young twigs to themselves' (Laurentian Ms., 3b, 21)

(8) *pokorivše ja podъ sę*
'having subdued them (under them)'. (Laurentian Ms., 8b, 30)

Other examples occur in religious texts (the Life of Savva, for example). Attestations are infrequent; examples (6) – (8) above are the only examples in the Laurentian Manuscript (Primary Chronicle), which, however, contains no examples of the genitive-accusative *sebe* after prepositions.

Genitive-accusative *sebe* occurs in even our earliest texts, as is shown in the following examples from the 11th century:

(9) *ašče priobręščetь vьsь mirъ. a sebe pogoubitь*
'if (he) gains the whole world, but forfeits himself' (Ostromir Gospel, 224b; Luke 9.25)

(10) *vy jeste opravьdajǫšče sebe prědъ čl(o)v(ě)ky*
'you are they-who-declare-themselves-just before men'. (Ostr. 112a; Luke 16.15)

(11) *podobajetь oubo öboje tvoriti ježe bo vračǫ vračǫi sebe*
'it is fitting to do both, as for a physician: heal thyself'. (Izbornik of 1076, leaf 93v, 6–8, page 444)

Problems of interpretation arise, similar to those that occur in analyzing the anaphoric genitive-accusative. Additional difficulty is created, however, by the relative infrequency of the reflexive accusative. Most clear examples of the genitive-accusative in the 11th-century texts seem to be contrastive or emphatic, like (9) and (11) above; however, example (10), which is attested in the same form in Old Church Slavonic (see Lunt 1974:142), is not emphatic.

By the 13th century, at least some texts show *sebe* as the normal accusative form in direct object position, for example:

(12) *oudariti sebe po vsę dьni*
'to strike oneself every day'. (Life of Nifont, page 253, 6–7)

Examples continue to be rare, however, and there is only one attestation in the Primary Chronicle of the Laurentian Manuscript:

(13)   *po čto gubite sebe*
       'why do you destroy yourselves?' (Laurentian Ms., 44c, 01)

This same text, while it has just this one example of *sebe*, also has no clear occurrences outside of prepositional phrases of a direct-object form *sę* that can be proved not to be a verbal particle, that is, the equivalent of the particle *-sja* in East Slavic today. The status of *sę* as pronoun or particle has tended to be fluid throughout the history of the Slavic languages. In Old Church Slavonic, *sę* resisted replacement by genitive *sebe* after supines and in negated constructions, where genitive rection was normal. In 13th- and 14th-century East Slavic writing, there is no clear evidence that *sę* outside of prepositional phrases is **ever** a pronoun and not a verbal particle. The genitive-accusative had penetrated into prepositional phrases by the 14th century if not earlier, and seems to have been completely generalized by the 15th century.

Because *sę* follows the same declensional pattern as the singular personal pronouns *mę* 'me' and *tę* 'you', its history with respect to the genitive-accusative might be expected to be the same as theirs (see section 3 of this chapter). However, *mę* and *tę* continue to be attested well after *sę* has ceased to have any pronominal function, showing up sporadically, at least as an archaism, through the 17th century. *Mene* and *tebe* apparently replace *mę* and *tę* generally only in the 14th century, and are conditioned by stress (see below) in texts where *sebe* has been completely generalized.

3. The Personal Pronouns.

None of the personal pronouns is very well attested, compared with the anaphoric pronoun *ego* (see Chapter Two). Neither writs and charters nor birchbark letters provide much information from before 1300, although, until the very end of the 13th century, the few attestations found are all of the old accusative forms. At the very end of the 13th century, there are a few possible genitive-accusative singulars in birchbark letters (see Savignac 1974:50 for a complete list), although even these are probably best interpreted as genitive case forms — for example, a direct object of *xotěti*, which is known to have governed the genitive, and an object of the preposition *za* in the meaning of 'on (my) behalf', which also frequently took the genitive. A Polock document from about 1300 has an apparent genitive-accusative second-person plural *vasъ*; however, the form in question is governed by *za*, and so may be a true genitive. The example reads as follows:

(14)   *a /ę/zъ klanęju sę i ... boga molju za vasъ děti svoě. aže budetъ poločaninъ čimъ*
       vinovatъ rižaninu ę za těmъ ne stoju
       'and I bow and pray to God for you my children. And if a Polockian has somehow committed an offense against someone from Riga, I do not support him'. (cited from Gribble 1973:135)

If *vasъ* is a genitive-accusative in (14), then it should, as the object of a preposition, represent a fairly late stage of genitive-accusative implementation, according to the general rule; however, *za*, because of its genitive rection, seems to have been exceptional in this respect. Moreover, the linguistic status of (14) is not entirely clear. Because it occurs in an episcopal letter, its language might be expected to be purely Slavonic; however, the conjunction *aže* 'if' in a purely Slavonic text ought to occur in the form *ašče* instead. In addition, it might be suggested that the forms of the first-person singular pronoun *ę* and *ęzъ* are non-Slavonic, as distinct from the Slavonic *azъ*. However, Worth (in press) has shown that the choice among these three forms is phonotactically, more than stylistically, conditioned in, at least, the Primary Chronicle (Laurentian text). His description can be extended (with minor adjustments) to cover the examples in (14) as well, suggesting that these forms are not reliable indicators of the style of this document.

The next genitive-accusative plurals are found in writs and charters beginning about 1341, and the old accusative forms disappear completely from legal language after the end of the 14th century. The first singular genitive-accusative in writs and charters is from 1368, and the genitive-accusative is the only regular accusative form by the end of the century. (A fairly accurate survey of these materials is found in Borkovskij 1949: 365–366.) However, the old accusative singular lingers on as an archaism, already rare in Unbegaun's corpus from the first half of the 16th century (Unbegaun 1935:364 ff.), but still found occasionally even in the 17th century (Cocron 1962:135). The general impression created by the writs and charters is that the plurals generally innovated the genitive-accusative before the singulars, with the 2nd person perhaps slightly ahead of the 1st person. As noted above, the documentation of the writs and charters is too sparse to be of much independent value, but does agree with evidence from other kinds of texts.

Religious texts and chronicles provide much more extensive documentation of the personal-pronoun forms, including some duals, beginning in the 11th century; as indicated in the previous two chapters, however, there are great difficulties in generalizing from this sort of documentation to contemporary non-Slavonic East Slavic. As noted below, in discussing example (27), there is some reason to class the Laurentian Manuscript Primary Chronicle (as well as at least large parts of other chronicles) more with religious texts than with secular ones, not only with respect to the anaphoric pronouns but also with respect to personal pronoun usage. As can be seen from Table 3–1, the statistical distribution of personal-pronoun accusative forms is about the same in the Primary Chronicle as it is in religious texts that are considerably older.

In religious and chronicle texts there is some evidence of a correlation of the singular genitive-accusative with sentential stress or emphasis, but the correlation is not very strong, and is not well supported in the plural or dual. The singular accusative forms are much better attested than the plurals, and the singular genitive-accusative is relatively much less frequent than the plural in all the texts examined, from the period up to the generalization of the genitive-accusative form. For religious and chronicle texts of which I have made a complete count, the distribution of the personal-pronoun genitive-accusative is summarized, in absolute figures, in Table 3–1. A complete survey of the same forms in the Suzdal Chronicle appears in Cohen 1976; an incomplete and not entirely accurate list of examples in the Synod Copy of the Novgorod Chronicle is given in Istrina 1923:155.

Table 3–1

Personal-Pronoun Genitive-Accusative Forms in Selected Religious and Chronicle Texts from before 1400, as Proportions of the Total Numbers of Accusative Personal-Pronoun Accusative Forms.

Singular

	1st Person	2nd Person	TOTAL
Izbornik 1076	2 / 21	2 / 71	4 / 92
Uspenskij Sb.	9 / 292	0 / 181	9 / 473
Nifont 1219	10 / 160	7 / 61	17 / 221
Savva (13th c.)	4 / 26	0 / 4	4 / 30
Laurentian Ms., Primary Chr.	8 / 89	6 / 61	14 / 150
TOTAL	33 / 588	15 / 378	48 / 966

Plural

	1st Person	2nd Person	TOTAL
Izbornik 1076	2 / 13	0 / 5	2 / 18
Uspenskij Sb.	19 / 124	6 / 69	25 / 193
Nifont 1219	4 / 45	3 / 9	7 / 54
Savva (13th c.)	3 / 7	5 / 6	8 / 13
Laurentian Ms., Primary Chr.	9 / 61	6 / 34	15 / 95
TOTAL	37 / 250	20 / 123	57 / 373
TOTAL	70 / 838	35 / 501	**105 / 1339**

In the singular, there seems to be a general tendency for the nongenitive accusative form to appear nearly entirely in unstressed position; there is, however, one exception to this rule in my corpus:

(15) *jako že sxrani enoxa… i potomъ noja… avrama… lota… moisěja… d(a)v(y)da … danila … tako i tę izbavitь ö/t/ neprijazni i ö/t/ sětii ego*
'as he saved Enoch … and then Noah … Abraham … Lot … Moses … David … Daniel … thus you too will he save from the Devil and his snares' (Laurentian Manuscript, leaf 17b, 31 to 18a, 5)

The text, from the Primary Chronicle, represents the Greek Patriarch's speech at Olga's baptism in 947.

Although the nongenitive accusative does not otherwise appear stressed in my corpus, the genitive-accusative appears both stressed and unstressed. With respect to the unstressed examples, it may be noted that there is some tendency, as with early examples of *jego*, for the genitive-accusative to appear modified or as the first member of a so-called double-object construction. Preposed objects are regularly genitive-accusative. A few examples can serve to illustrate the general range of occurrences:

(16) *da znajǫtь tebe jedinogo istinьnaago b(og)a*
'that they know thee the only true god' (Ostromir Gospel, 174a; John 17.3)

(17) *da razidetь sę kъždo vъ svoja i mene jedinogo ostavite*
'that you will all be scattered and will leave me alone' (Ibid., 52a; John 16.32 erroneously labeled John 14.32 in Vostokov)

(18) *vidite jako ne sebě jedinomou troudixъ sę. nъ i vsěmъ iskouštiimъ mene.*
'you see that I did not labor for myself alone, but also for all who try me'. (Izbornik of 1076, leaf 84, 4–7, page 425)

(Example (18) is unusual in having an apparently unmotivated genitive-accusative *mene*. It is, however, possible that this is a true genitive, rather than a genitive-accusative. The example is interesting also because it shows the genitive-accusative, if such it be, governed by a participle; as noted, there is a strong tendency for *jego* to appear first in participial constructions, but a comparable tendency is not well documented for the personal pronouns. The example is included here partly because of the rarity of genitive-accusatives in the Izbornik of 1076 — 5, including this one; another example from this text appears below at (30).)

(19) *mene oskvъrьnьšouju sę ömyi*
'cleanse me, who have defiled himself' (Uspenskij Sbornik, 196a, 7–9)

(20) *i mene čьtoutь i tebe slavętь*
'they both honor me and glorify thee' (Ibid., 101d, 1–2)

(21) *gl(agol)a ei bl(a)g(oslo)vi mę m(a)ti padъši že i öna na nogou jego gl(agol)še ty mene bl(a)g(oslo)vi.. g(ospod)i o(t)če moi*

'he said to her: bless me, mother; and she, falling at his feet, said: it must be you who bless me, lord, my father'. (Ibid., 118b, 29 ff.)

(My corpus of 300 examples of *mene* and *mę* from the Uspenskij Sbornik includes only 9 examples of genitive-accusatives, and all 9 are of the general sort illustrated in (19) – (21) above: contrastive or preposed.)

(22) *to tebe byxъ vъ sii ča/s/ vъrglъ dolou i sъkroušilъ tę*
'then would I have thrown you down and destroyed you' (Life of Nifont, page 368, lines 17–18)

(23) *oukrasi mene vъ zvězdy město s(vę)tymъ d(u)x(o)mъ prosvěti mę i vъ öblaka město öblěci mę.*
'make me bright in the place of a star, enlighten me with the holy spirit, and don me like a cloud'. (Ibid., page 271.4–6)

(The Life of Nifont uses the genitive-accusative more freely than the texts cited immediately above, and the motivation for the occurrence of *mene* instead of *mę* is, as shown by these examples, less obvious. The other examples — a total of 17 *tebe* and *mene* out of a corpus of 221 — are more clearly emphatic or contrastive.)

(24) *ötpousti ju ... mene že ... ouderža*
'dismissed her ... but me ... he detained' (Life of Savva the Enlightened, 437.15–16)

(25) *bl(a)g(oslo)vi o(t)ca i m(a)t(e)rъ i mene*
'he blessed the father and the mother and me' (Ibid., 439.3–4)

(26) *aže togo oubiete oubiïte mene pereže*
'if you kill him, kill me first' (Synod Ms. 134, 10)

(27) *izъbъjutъ družinu moju i mene*
'they will kill my retinue and me'. (Laurentian Ms., 22a, 12)

(Example (27) is one of the few personal-pronoun genitive-accusatives in the Primary Chronicle of the Laurentian Manuscript that is not in a highly Slavonic environment, if not in a direct citation of liturgical sources. Thus, there is some basis for suggesting that the conservative character of the genitive-accusative in this text, already noted with respect to the anaphoric pronoun forms, is not restricted to them. A similar tendency is noted for animal-referential nouns, in Chapter Four, §3.)

As noted above, neither the plural nor the dual is so well attested as the singular; however, our documentation is adequate for tracing general lines of development. In addition to the figures presented in Table 1, we may note that, according to Vostokov's word list, the genitive-accusative *vasъ* does not occur in the Ostromir Gospel (or, rather, occurs, according to Vostokov, only under negation (!)); accusative plural *nasъ* occurs only once, replacing an expected dual in the speech of one of the two thieves crucified on either side of Christ:

(28) *ašče ty jesi x(risto)sъ. sp(a)si sę samъ i nasъ*
      'if you are Christ, save yourself and us' (Ostromir Gospel, 192a; Luke 23.39)

As this example suggests, the dual personal pronouns are unstable in our earliest texts. The old dual accusatives *na* and *va* are very poorly attested, and are replaced by dual or plural genitive-accusatives even in texts such as the Ostromir where the dual is otherwise well preserved, and where the plural personal pronouns generally show the old accusative rather than the genitive-accusative. On the other hand, the Izbornik of 1076, which has one occurrence each of the nominative-accusative dual *va* and the genitive-accusative *vaju*, uses the plural *vy* instead of *va* as the dual nominative.

There is not any overwhelming evidence of any correlation between stress and the choice of the plural genitive-accusative, and it is not at all clear that different texts reflect the same usage. The old accusative plurals *ny* and *vy* occur apparently stressed 3 times in my corpus:

(29) *ašče mene izgъnašę i vy iždenǫtь*
      'if they persecuted me, they will persecute you' (Ostromir Gospel 170a; John 15.20)
(30) *iže vy xoulitь mene xoulitь*
      'he who reviles you, reviles me' (Izbornik of 1076, leaf 258v, 8–10, page 666)
(31) *vy li i prijaste na to město ili onъ vasъ. oni že rěša onъ ny prijatъ*
      'Did you accept him into that place, or (did) he (accept) you? And they said: he accepted us'. (Life of Savva, 93.12–14)

Although the other examples of *vy* and *ny* in these texts are not stressed, neither, so far as I can tell, are the examples of *nasъ* and *vasъ*. In other texts, *vy* and *ny* are unstressed and *vasъ* and *nasъ* occur both unstressed and contrastively or emphatically stressed.

Chapter Four. The Genitive-Accusative in the History of Noun and Adjective Declension.

1. The Historical Relation between the Pronoun Genitive-Accusative and the Genitive-Accusative in Nouns and Adjectives.

The historical relation between noun and adjective genitive-accusative syncretism, on the one hand, and the corresponding pronoun syncretism, on the other, is not entirely clear. Both main types of syncretism originated in prehistoric Slavic, and there are several theories of how they were related in their earliest stages.

According to Meillet (1897), the genitive-accusative originated in pronoun declension and spread from there to nouns and adjectives. Among the pronouns, the indefinite animate *kъto* is commonly taken to be the starting point (see Vondrák 1898, Meillet 1934/1965:442), since the only attested accusative of *kъto* anywhere in Slavic is the genitive-accusative *kogo*. However, according to Meillet (1897), the anaphoric genitive-accusative *ego* was not extended into accusative usage from the genitive, but was an original genitive-accusative; moreover, Meillet considered this form important for the rise of the genitive-accusative in adjectives and nouns, for the following reason. Since *ego* was a genitive-accusative, the long-form (definite) adjectives also had a genitive-accusative, because they were formed from short-form (indefinite) adjectives to which were added the corresponding forms of the anaphoric pronouns. Thus, the rise of the adjectival genitive-accusative occurred more or less mechanically, through the direct influence of the earlier anaphoric genitive-accusative. Nouns modified by long-form adjectives then tended to acquire the genitive-accusative as a result of their influence. Meillet supports his theory with the fact that the earliest noun genitive-accusatives were in fact mainly definite; this may seem to suggest the influence of the definite adjectives. Nevertheless, Meillet's theory has not been universally accepted, for several reasons.

The original accusative status of the pronoun genitive-accusative was never established, and there is evidence against it (Berneker 1904:370–375). In addition, the tendency of the early noun genitive-accusatives to be definite need not reflect the influence of definite adjectives, since the same tendency is found much later, in noun classes that began to acquire the genitive-accusative only long after adjective declension had ceased marking definiteness (see below and Chapter Five). Finally, no such direct influence need have been exerted, according to the view of Thomson and others who consider the noun and adjective genitive-accusative to have been strongly motivated by communicative necessity. Since, in this view, the genitive-accusative in nouns and adjectives (but not in pronouns) served to redifferentiate accusative object forms from nominative subjects, the impetus for the noun genitive-accusative must lie in the syntax and declension of the nouns themselves, whereas the pronouns, if they developed the genitive-accusative earlier, can have served only as a rough analogical model. In Thomson's theory, Meillet's more mechanical description of the rise of the genitive-accusative is irrelevant, because there were no such mechanisms in other languages that, according to Thomson, also developed subject-object differentiation. (Thomson 1909 compares the Slavic development with similar developments in Romance, Baltic, Ossetian, and Armenian.) Meillet himself seems to have accepted Thomson's theory (Meillet 1934/1965:406).

Because the innovation of Slavic genitive-accusative syncretism is inaccessible to historical documentation, the controversy over the original relations among the different classes of the syncretism is unlikely ever to be fully resolved. Within East Slavic, noun and adjective genitive-accusative syncretism apparently developed independently of the pronominal syncretism, although there are important similarities between them. Like pronoun genitive-accusatives, the noun and adjective genitive-accusative seems to have developed by means of the reanalysis of syntactic genitive objects, since it tends to appear first in environments where a syntactic genitive object is at least marginally acceptable: after verbs (such as *viděti*) either in the process of losing genitive rection or synonymous with verbs that govern the genitive, in constructions containing a negated element, and in participial constructions. Direct-object accusatives appear frequently in the genitive-accusative at an earlier period than do accusative objects of prepositions. All of these tendencies are discussed in Chapter Two and will not be treated separately here. In addition, noun and adjective genitive-accusative syncretism has two special restrictions that distinguish it from the pronominal genitive-accusative, although even these characteristically nominal restrictions on the genitive-accusative are at least marginally relevant to the pronoun development as well.

The first of these special conditions is that noun and adjective genitive-accusative syncretism is and has always been restricted nearly entirely to the declension of nouns referring to animate beings, along with adjectives modifying such nouns. For the most part, nominal genitive-accusative syncretism applied first to human-referential nouns and their modifiers, and only later to nouns referring to animals (see below). The second restriction is that nouns, unlike pronouns, acquired genitive-accusative syncretism only in paradigms that had previously established nominative-accusative syncretism. The combined effect of these restrictions was for genitive-accusative syncretism in nouns, but not in pronouns, to create a set of paired declension classes, such that otherwise inflexionally equivalent nouns have either genitive-accusative or nominative-accusative syncretism, depending on their reference. However, even with respect to these two conditions, the distinction between pronominal and nominal syncretism is less than absolute.

The requirement that a genitive-accusative form be referentially animate (or human) is of obvious importance for noun and adjective genitive-accusative syncretism; this requirement was not directly relevant to pronominal genitive-accusative syncretism, but the distinction between the two main classes of genitive-accusative is less clear in this respect than such a simple statement may seem to imply. In the first place, all Slavic languages have some referential inanimates that also take a genitive-accusative (in the singular only) and the frequency of such examples in Old Church Slavonic (see Vaillant 1964:177) tends to suggest that the referential conditions on noun genitive-accusative syncretism stabilized only well after the syncretism itself had begun to occur. In East Slavic, the genitive-accusative regularly occurred only on personal nouns, not on animal nouns, up to the 17th century, but, there too, there is considerable vacillation from the 14th century onward (see below). Thus, an "animacy condition" on nominal genitive-accusative syncretism represents a simplification of the facts. On the other hand, first- and second-person pronouns always have animate (usually human) antecedents, and, more interestingly, the great majority of the early occurrences of the anaphoric genitive-accusative *ego* were also human in reference (for statistics on the Suzdal Chronicle, see Cohen 1976). Neither of these facts, however, has anything directly to do with the genitive-accusative. With respect to the personal pronouns, this is of course obvious, but the anaphoric genitive-accusative is a slightly subtler problem. In the first place, most anaphoric pronouns in the texts in my corpus are referentially human, for reasons probably having to do with discourse structure: anaphora tends to apply to elements well established in discourse, and the elements that tend to become well-established topics of discourse usually refer to things that interest speakers — hence, human beings are more likely to appear in anaphoric forms than are, say, toponyms or plant names (see Kuno 1975). In the second place, the inanimate anaphoric pronouns in my texts occur disproportionately rarely in the complex syntactic environments that favor the genitive-accusative (see Chapter Two); the few examples of inanimate genitive-accusative *ego* that I have found (see e.g. Chapter Two, examples (57) and (71)) are unusual not only because of their inanimate reference but also because they are direct objects of personal verb forms — a poor environment for the anaphoric genitive-accusative in the texts where they occur. It is, for this reason, surprising that some of the earliest occurrences of genitive-accusative *ego* in non-

Slavonic texts are in fact referentially inanimate, as in, for example, the Smolensk treaty of 1229, and, correspondingly, there is no reason to posit an "animacy" or "personhood" restriction on the anaphoric genitive-accusative itself. Purely statistically, however, the anaphoric genitive-accusative was not much less likely to be referentially animate than was a noun genitive-accusative; only the status of this correlation seems to be different in the two classes of syncretism.

The second distinguishing characteristic of nominal and adjectival genitive-accusative syncretism is that it arose only in paradigms that had previously established nominative-accusative syncretism. This fact has been emphasized by Thomson (1908) and others who treat the genitive-accusative as a therapeutic response to nominative-accusative syncretism; this functionalist approach has had to separate noun from pronoun genitive-accusative syncretism, since the latter has obviously spread into paradigms lacking nominative-accusative syncretism. However, in this respect, as with respect to the animacy condition, the difference between nouns and pronouns is less clear than it might seem to be. Among the personal, anaphoric and relative pronoun declensions, it seems likely that the earliest genitive-accusatives were *vasъ* (second person plural) and *egože* (masculine singular relative pronoun). The forms they replaced, *vy* and *iže* respectively, were nominative-accusative syncretic. Documentation is not entirely clear, but Grünenthal (1910:358) noted that *egože* in Old Church Slavonic was the regular masculine accusative singular, whereas *ego* was much less common as the accusative anaphoric pronoun. In early East Slavic, the relative *iže* occurs only in Slavonic environments, and *egože* is the only regularly occurring masculine singular accusative in direct-object position. This form provides a plausible model for anaphoric genitive-accusative *ego*. The anaphoric and relative pronoun paradigms are identical except for the presence of *že* in the relative pronoun and the lack of a nominative in the anaphoric pronoun; the genitive-accusative *ego* appears first in texts that use *egože* as a relative. In addition, the corresponding anaphoric plural *ixъ* in at least one long text, the Suzdal Chronicle, occurs relatively frequently, but only in the part of the text that also makes use of the unusual accusative plural form *i* — syncretic not only with the accusative masculine singular, but also with the hypothetical (but nonoccurrent) nominative plural. Thus, there is some evidence that nominative-accusative syncretism influenced the rise of the anaphoric genitive-accusative. The personal pronouns are textually infrequent, especially in the plural, making it hard to analyze the early history of the East Slavic genitive-accusative in these forms. Here, too, however, there is at least some support for the idea that the genitive-accusative developed most rapidly in the paradigm that had nominative-accusative syncretism, namely the second-person plural (see Chapter Three). Thus, nominative-accusative syncretism was at least marginally a positive factor, favoring the genitive-accusative in pronouns. Just as this factor has been neglected in studying the history of the pronouns, its importance has probably been overestimated in the history of the nouns. Nominative-accusative syncretism in noun paradigms was never by itself sufficient to condition genitive-accusative syncretism. Declension classes lacking a singular genitive-accusative did not develop it in the plural, even if the plural was nominative-accusative syncretic; thus, feminine and neuter plurals acquired a genitive-accusative only after the plural had lost its original gender distinctions, even though feminine and neuter plurals (but not singulars) had always been nominative-accusative syncretic. This indicates that the rise of the genitive-accusative depended not just on whether or not there were a nominative-accusative in the paradigm, but also on the relation of the paradigm in question to the rest of the declensional system. A different fact pointing in the same direction is that the genitive-accusative in the masculine singular was limited to the old o-stems; human-referential nouns such as *synъ* and *gostь*, belonging to other declension classes, acquired genitive-accusative syncretism only insofar as they became o-stems, even though they were nominative-accusative syncretic without assimilating to the o-stems. On the other hand, we occasionally find in Old Church Slavonic personal feminine nouns with genitive-accusatives, although their normal accusatives were not syncretic — e.g. *matere* 'mother (gen.-acc.)' for expected *materь* (see Lunt 1974:62). Thus, nominative-accusative syncretism was a strong positive factor in the rise of the genitive-accusative (and the need for nominative-accusative differentiation is attested in other developments, as we will see below); nevertheless, it is an oversimplification to analyze the genitive-accusative as a response to just this one phenomenon.

We noted above that there are a number of minor conditions shared by pronominal and noun/adjective genitive-accusative syncretism. Here we have examined the two major phenomena that seem most clearly to differentiate them, and we find that the differences, even here, are less sharp than may at first appear. However, this does not mean that the two main types of genitive-accusative can usefully be treated as the same thing. First of all, neither animacy nor nominative-accusative syncretism plays exactly the same role in the two different kinds of genitive-accusative; in addition, the chronology of the two classes is rather different. The anaphoric masculine singular and plural genitive-accusative was completely generalized by 1400, at least outside obviously archaic texts; although the neuter and feminine genitive-accusatives were generalized later, they are well attested from the 15th century on. The personal pronouns also generalized the genitive-accusative by the end of the 14th century. Although the singular anaphoric pronoun and the plural personal pronouns seem at first to generalize the genitive-accusative particularly rapidly, there is, as we have seen (Chapters Two and Three), considerable overlap. In general, the pronouns generalized the genitive-accusative relatively rapidly, relatively early, and without much clear division into chronologically distinct stages of extension from one form class to another. The nouns, on the other hand, acquired the genitive-accusative more slowly and gradually, with extensive variability in usage throughout the pre-modern East Slavic period. There was a clear division into stages of the noun genitive-accusative, according to number (singular first) and according to referentiality (human-referential before other animates). Human-referential masculine singular nouns and their modifiers provided the core of early noun and adjective genitive-accusative syncretism, with occasional occurrences of plural genitive-accusatives or of genitive-accusative animal nouns. By the end of the 15th century, the genitive-accusative had extended to masculine plural personal nouns (see Unbegaun 1935:228–236 and below), and, from there, began to extend to human-reference feminines and finally to other animates. Plural animal-noun genitive-accusatives do not occur before the 16th century. In general, the referential and nominative-accusative syncretism conditions, discussed above, provided a kind of braking effect on the generalization of the noun genitive-accusative: the genitive-accusative expanded only when the conditions were relaxed (from the condition that the accusative form refer to a human being), or when the range of the already existing condition was expanded (through the growth of nominative-accusative syncretism or the loss of gender distinctions in the plurals). There was no similar stepwise implementation of the genitive-accusative in pronouns.

Thus, animacy and nominative-accusative syncretism served as principles of division of the nouns into subclasses, for the purpose of implementing genitive-accusative syncretism. That such a function should have been served more consistently in noun than in pronoun declension probably is at least partly the result of the much broader scale of the noun syncretism, affecting as it did a large and constantly growing class of elements. The fact that the two conditions under discussion consistently served to discriminate the nouns that acquired genitive-accusative syncretism from those that did not is the historical analogue of the fact that the genitive-accusative in modern Russian distinguishes subclasses of nouns from one another — in other words, that it marks (in a broad sense — see Chapter Six) the subgender of animate nouns. In that sense, it is not strictly accurate to speak of the development in Russian of a subgender or category of animacy, implying that there was a time when the language lacked such a subcategory. On the contrary, the genitive-accusative throughout its history in Russian noun declension has *always* served as a marker of a "subgender", whose range, however, expanded over time. (In our present discussion, the words "subgender" or "gender" are used synonymously with "noun class" or "classification". In fact, this usage will be codified somewhat when we look at the modern status of animacy as a subgender in Russian — see Chapter Six.) Thus, one main difference between the two kinds of genitive-accusative is exactly the same historically as it is synchronically: one type of genitive-accusative (what we have been calling the pronominal type) has been generalized, whereas the other type (found in the declension of nouns, their modifiers, and the relative pronoun) has served as a marker of noun classification.

The function of the genitive-accusative as a noun classifier has been neglected in accounts of the history of the genitive-accusative, although its synchronic function as a gender marker is well known. Historical studies have focused on either phonological or syntactic aspects of the rise of the genitive-accusative, concentrating on the processes that led to the erosion of Indoeuropean nominative-accusative case differentiation and on the value of the genitive-accusative as a marker of grammatical relations. However, the genitive-accusative is first of all a phenomenon neither of phonology nor of syntax, but of inflexional morphology, and its historical context was, most immediately, the collapse of the inherited Indoeuropean declensional system and its replacement by the modern Russian one.

2. Changes in Old Russian Noun Declension.

As is well known, Modern Russian nouns show a strong correlation among semantic gender criteria (sex reference), syntactic gender (as manifested in agreement patterns), and what, following Zaliznjak (1967:138–149), can be called "morphological gender" (see also Peškovskij 1928/1956:93–94). For example, nouns referring to women typically belong to the declension class in -*a*, which typically also triggers a unified "feminine" agreement pattern in adjectives, verbs, and other agreeing forms. There are several well known exceptions to the general rule. One type is the nouns with augmentative or diminutive suffixes, which do not determine syntactic gender, although they may determine inflexional class. (See Zaliznjak 1967:148–149.) Another type of problem arises with some human-referential nouns, for example the male-referential nouns of the -*a* declension type; atypical gender patterns of human-referential nouns are discussed in Chapter Six. In addition, there is a fairly substantial number of borrowed words, mainly inanimate, whose gender has been historically unstable (see Stone 1978:73–82). However, the existence of such exceptional situations does not alter the fact that, on the whole, the mapping between inflexional and agreement patterns in Modern Russian is fairly simple and exact. This simplicity arose only as a result of historical changes in Russian declension: individual nouns and groups of nouns migrated from one class to another, sometimes several times, while the Old Russian noun classes themselves became increasingly indistinguishable from one another, and their internal organization was modified. The tendency was for the many changes in noun inflexion to simplify the relation between (syntactic and semantic) noun gender, on the one hand, and, on the other, gender morphology. Gender was an important mode of organization for the inflexional changes as they occurred. Thus, for example, masculine i-stems tended to drift into the o-stem type of declension, leaving behind in the i-stems not only original i-stem feminines but also some feminine nouns that had migrated to the i-stems from more archaic declension classes: *ljuby* 'love' and *svekry* 'mother-in-law' from the old ū-stems and *mati* 'mother' and *doči* 'daughter' from the old consonant stems. In addition, the reorganization of Old Russian noun classes also made use, sometimes ephemeral, of inanimacy and personal (or animate) reference. Thus, for example, among i-stem masculines, the first nouns to shift to the o-stem type of declension were animate: *zjatъ* 'son-in-law' *tatъ* 'thief', *golubъ* 'dove', and *červъ* 'worm' (see Unbegaun 1935:64–78). On the other hand, the personal-reference nouns *svekry, mati,* and *doči* resisted nominative-accusative syncretism long after other old ū- and consonant-stems had completely assimilated to the i-stems and adopted the nominative-accusative syncretism characteristic of their new declension class (Unbegaun 1935:68, Cocron 1962:49). Thus, personal (or animate) reference evidently affected the migration of nouns from one declension class to another, and apparently retarded the development of nominative-accusative syncretism in some nouns. Conversely, the migration of human-referential masculine nouns from the i-stems to the o-stems (as well as the transfer of *synъ* 'son', the only personal-reference u-stem, from the u-stems to the o-stems) can be interpreted as evidence of a tendency for personal-reference nouns to reject nominative-accusative syncretism and move to declension classes with genitive-accusative syncretism instead. In general, the presence or absence of nominative-accusative or genitive-accusative syncretism in noun paradigms seems to have been an important factor affecting the assimilation of nouns to new declension classes; personal-reference (and animate) nouns tended to assimilate to paradigms with genitive-accusative syncretism and tended not to develop nominative-accusative syncretism. This picture is somewhat obscured by the fact that nouns in the process of assimilating to the o-stem declension class — notably *synъ* and *gostъ* — retained a nominative-accusative form well after personal o-stems in general were genitive-accusative syncretic; this situation, however, is only a transitional stage in the assimilation of these nouns to the o-stem (genitive-accusative) pattern.

More important than the transfer of individual lexical items from one class to another was the actual reorganization of the noun classes themselves. In practice, it is sometimes difficult to distinguish the two types of change. In addition, paradigmatic reorganization itself was structurally of at least two main types (integration of originally distinct declension classes and realignment of relations among endings within a single paradigm), but these two types of change are also highly interdependent.

One of the most salient examples of this interdependency is the history of the endings that originally characterized the genitive and locative singular of u-stem nouns. As is well known, the u-stems began to fall together even prehistorically with the much more numerous o-stem class. Except for one human-referential noun *synъ* 'son' and one animal noun *volъ* 'ox', the original u-stems were all inanimate; as the u-stem declension type as such disappeared, it left traces in the form of subclasses of inanimate nouns that took distinct genitive and/or locative singular endings (namely, the original u-stem endings), although otherwise conforming to the o-stem pattern. These classes of nouns became quite large in Old Russian, and included inanimate masculine nouns of the original o-stem type. In Modern Russian, these same original u-stem endings have become markers of the new "second genitive" and "second locative" cases (see Jakobson 1958/1971, Zaliznjak 1967:43–46, Panov 1968:175–199). Although the number of nouns taking these special endings is limited, and the "second genitive", in particular, seems to be receding, nevertheless the history of the u-stem genitive and locative singular endings is a phenomenon belonging both to the area of integration of disparate declension types and to that of the ultimate modification of the case system internal to the innovated paradigm.

The example of the u-stem genitive and locative singular is particularly relevant to our present discussion, for two reasons. First, and most important, it illustrates the very general scope of the changes undergone by the Old Russian declensional system: out of what had been two distinct declension classes there emerged a single new declension class, whose membership included nouns of different subtypes, including subtypes that took the old u-stem desinences, and, most strikingly, there also emerged two new cases, obviously one of the most important changes possible in a declensional system. Thus, the apparently low-level reshuffling of inflexional patterns had a quite drastic result affecting the whole structure of Russian inflexion. More important than any single event in the history of Old Russian declension classes was precisely the instability of the whole system, which was so strikingly open to innovation. In such a labile situation, especially if it is viewed at a considerable historical remove, it is futile to try to reconstruct simple and completely determinate cause-and-effect relations between one event and another. For this reason, the classical hypothesis according to which the spread of the genitive-accusative was caused by systematic ambiguity can at best be taken as a reasonable statement about what was likely to have contributed to the growth of the genitive-accusative, in otherwise favorable circumstances. It is impossible to decide whether, for example, the problem of ambiguity would not have had another solution, except for simultaneous pressure to create a reasonably efficient classificatory system for nouns, to replace the one that had in some instances literally worn out.

A second aspect of the later history of the u-stem genitive and locative singular endings is their association with referential inanimacy. We will see below other instances of animacy, inanimacy, or personhood becoming an important mode of organization for Old Russian nouns; we have already noted the function of these factors as a temporary mode of ordering migration of nouns from one declension class to another. These functions of animacy/inanimacy/personhood are apparently independent of the growth of the genitive-accusative; thus, the growth of genitive-accusative syncretism is only one example of a more general tendency for the changing Old Russian declensional system to exploit referential animacy/personhood as a basis for organizing paradigms. Although why noun reference should have become so important is a matter of speculation, it is likely that it provided a unique point of stability in an otherwise confused situation: it is, after all, clear, for any given noun, whether it is referentially animate or inanimate, or refers to human beings, whereas it was apparently often not clear at all what formal properties could be associated with it. Thus, the extension of genitive-accusative syncretism, conditioned by personhood or animacy, was likely to have been facilitated by the more general tendency of the contemporary noun classification system to exploit noun reference.

Aside from the u-stem genitive and locative singular endings and their assimilation into the newly integrated masculine declensional pattern, the main changes in noun declension in Old Russian were in the plural. Here, change affected all case forms. In the oblique cases, the original feminine a-stem endings -am, -ami, and -ax became generalized as the dative, instrumental, and locative plural respectively for nouns of all three genders. This development, attested from the 13th century on but completed as late as the 18th century, was so complex and affected by so many different factors in the three cases involved, that Kiparsky (1963–1975:2.54 ff.) declines even to treat

them under a common heading.[1] Referential animacy and personhood seem
not to have been relevant to the implementation of this change. One of its most
obvious results was the loss of the morphological expression of gender in the
plural of the three cases affected; plural nouns had of course never expressed
syntactic gender in these cases, since there had never been any gender distinctions among agreeing modifiers. Thus, the extension of -*am*, -*ami*, and -*ax*
represented, among other things, a consolidation of gender neutralization in
Russian plural noun declension, resulting in increased isomorphism between
morphological and syntactic gender patterns and in weakened expression of
the original sex-based gender distinctions in the plural. The extension of
genitive-accusative syncretism to masculine plural nouns on the whole preceded the extension of the feminine oblique desinences to nonfeminines; on
the other hand, the extension of the genitive-accusative to nonmasculine
animates in general followed the loss of the oblique gender distinctions. Thus,
the extension of the plural genitive-accusative to nonmasculine nouns is
correlated with the more general loss of plural gender distinctions, as shown in
the extension of -*am*, -*ami*, -*ax* to nonfeminines.

The extension of the genitive-accusative to masculine plural nouns tended,
of course, to make the plural noun classification system symmetrical with the
pattern in the singular; however, the generalization of the feminine oblique
desinences tended in the opposite direction, and this relative independence of
plural from singular declension in Russian nouns was further supported by the
later extension of the genitive-accusative to feminine and neuter plurals. Thus,
one function of this last development was to help articulate the asymmetric
relation of plural to singular declension as well as the unification of plural
noun classification patterns across both oblique and direct cases. Somewhat
more generally, the later history of genitive-accusative syncretism in nouns
advanced the status of the plural, and of the number category, in Russian, and
represented a further consolidation of the loss of plural gender already found
in the extension of the feminine dative, instrumental, and locative desinences
to nonfeminine nouns.

The most important change in the plural direct cases, and the change most
often discussed in relation to the genitive-accusative, is the development of
nominative-accusative syncretism in masculine nouns, which originally differed from nouns of other genders in having distinct nominative and accusative plural forms. We have already discussed the relation between nominative-
accusative and genitive-accusative syncretism (see §1).

The "hard" o-stem declension originally had an accusative plural ending -*y*
and a nominative -*i*, and the nominative -*i* conditioned mutation in stem-final
velar consonants. Thus, for example, the nominative plural of *bogъ* 'god' was

bozi, and the accusative plural was *bogy*. Russian declension in general rejected consonant mutations, and *y* and *i* had early become variants of a single phoneme, which always took the form *i* after velars. As a result there arose the Modern Russian nominative plural *bogi*, usually said to represent a substitution of the old accusative for the nominative. For inanimate nouns, such as *sapogъ* 'boot', the result was nominative-accusative plural case syncretism — *sapogi* for nominative and accusative, instead of the Old Russian *sapozi* vs. *sapogy*. For animate nouns, nominative-accusative syncretism is not found in Modern Russian, because genitive-accusative syncretism led to the loss of the old accusative plural hence nominative *bogi* vs. genitive and accusative *bogov*.

As noted by Šaxmatov (1910–1911/1957/1976:226–233) and many others, there was a sporadic retention of the old nominative form, but only among human-referential (or supernatural) nouns. In the modern language, there are only a very few examples — *čerti* 'devils', *sosedi* 'neighbors', and (archaic) *xolopi* 'serfs, servile people' — and they have extended the "softened" stem-final consonant to the whole plural declension, instead of retaining it as a nominative-case marker. Šaxmatov also notes (op. cit., 231) a few dialectal relics of the old nominative among inanimates, but points out that these nouns also occur with genitive-accusatives in the singular — card names, for example, such as *kresti* 'clubs' instead of standard *trefy*. In Old Russian, however, the late retention of the old nominative plural in human-referential nouns was rather widespread. In general, the nominative and accusative plural had fallen together completely by the 15th century, and yet even in the 16th century (and later), Unbegaun (1935:155–159) notes rather extensive use of the old nominative, albeit as an archaism, for human-referential nouns. In addition, the nominative plural -*e* (originally from consonant-stem nouns) also was preserved in a small set of human-referential nouns, where it occurs even in Modern Russian, in words such as *graždane* 'citizens' (see Zaliznjak 1967:228 for a complete list). In Old Russian, there was also a brief but quite extensive expansion of the nominative plural -*ove*, originally from the u-stems. It is perhaps surprising that the u-stem nominative plural should become, as it briefly did, a characteristically human-referential ending, since, as we have seen, the only human-referential noun among the original u-stems was *synъ* 'son'; however, -*ove* was very widespread as a nominative plural ending for human nouns from the 14th through 16th centuries, mainly in southern and southwestern documents and also in Slavonic documents from other areas (Filin 1972:390–394, Unbegaun 1935:159–162). There is thus abundant evidence of the resistance of human-referential nouns to the loss of the old nominative plural.

There is some reason to try to posit a direct link between the rise of the masculine plural genitive-accusative and the late retention of the old nominative plural in human-referential noun declension. Since, as we have seen, genitive-accusative syncretism in nouns is widely agreed to have occurred only in declensions already characterized by nominative-accusative syncretism, it is to be expected that nominative-accusative syncretism chronologically preceded genitive-accusative syncretism, and that the relatively late implementation of the plural genitive-accusative (15th century and later) can be attributed to the relatively late development of nominative-accusative syncretism (13th–14th centuries); for a representative statement of this point of view see Kuznecov (1965:224). Although this expectation is generally correct, certain caveats are required.

First, the retention of the old nominative case form did not necessarily mean that nominative-accusative syncretism did not occur, since the old nominative form could come to occur as an accusative as well (Unbegaun 1935:162); however, for the o-stem declension class this confusion seems to have been relatively late, after the nominative form had become artificial. In the "soft" declension type, the syncretic nominative-accusative actually is the same as the old nominative, and it was the old accusative that was lost, for animates and inanimates alike. Thus, retention of the old nominative need not entail keeping distinct nominative and accusative forms.

A special situation is represented by the expansion of the nominative plural form -*ove*. This ending occurred very widely in the East Slavic geographic area where the genitive-accusative expanded most slowly — in the south and southwest. The nominative -*ove* was not a long-established form whose presence impeded the progress of the innovative genitive-accusative; rather, they were both innovations competing in the same paradigm. Although the genitive-accusative was retained and -*ove* lost in both Russian and Ukrainian, the decline of -*ove* in 17th-century Ukrainian was apparently late enough to impede the implementation of the Ukrainian noun plural genitive-accusative. Unbegaun (1935:159–162) reports that -*ove* in his corpus occurs only in nouns that also had the plural genitive-accusative; also, however, according to Unbegaun, -*ove* in this corpus is nearly entirely an artificial form, characteristically noncolloquial and Slavonic, as it nearly invariably was outside the south and southwest. It is therefore likely that -*ove* was imposed for stylistic reasons on paradigms already marked as human-referential by the presence of the genitive-accusative.

Finally, it should be noted that Šaxmatov's analysis of the relation between the nominative-accusative and the genitive-accusative must be rejected, although it raises some interesting problems. According to Šaxmatov, the

reason for the resistence of animate nouns to nominative-accusative syncretism was that this type of syncretism involved substituting the old accusative
for the nominative; for animate nouns, such a substitution was impeded by the
rise of the genitive-accusative, which eliminated the accusatives that would
otherwise have been input for this rule. Šaxmatov does not explain why, in his
view, if genitive-accusative syncretism preceded nominative-accusative syncretism, the latter would not have occurred anyway, resulting in nominative-
accusative-genitive syncretism. Šaxmatov is wrong in viewing nominative-
accusative syncretism as simply a substitution of one form for another,
ignoring the motivation (and hence the limitations) of the change. He apparently does not differentiate among the various declension types: it was only the
"hard" o-stems that in fact show any accusative-for-nominative substitution
at all. He does not account for the extension of the old nominatives into
accusative usage. Most strikingly, he ignores his own view of the relative
chronology of the two changes: the genitive-accusative cannot have 'bled' off
the input to the nominative-accusative syncretism rule, if the nominative-
accusative syncretism occurred first, as it did. However, Šaxmatov's analysis
does raise the interesting problem of how to describe the interaction of the two
kinds of syncretism. Usually, as we have seen, the genitive-accusative is viewed
as a response to nominative-accusative syncretism, which both began and
completed its implementation earlier than genitive-accusative syncretism.
However, the plural genitive-accusative began to appear in the 14th century,
while the plural paradigms were still in the process of implementing
nominative-accusative syncretism, and, moreover, the last words to accept
nominative-accusative syncretism were indeed the personal nouns that were
the targets of genitive-accusative syncretism. Consequently, without tracing
the history of a large number of individual forms, it is impossible to know
whether there ever arose any well-defined stage in the history of Old Russian
declension when masculine human-referential nouns regularly had nominative-accusative syncretism. It is an unexplored possibility that, instead of a
clear progression from a nonsyncretic accusative to a nominative-accusative
syncretic form to a genitive-accusative, there was a period of considerable
variation, when all three paradigms may have co-existed. In such circumstances, the extension of the genitive-accusative from the singular to the plural of
masculine human-referential nouns would obviously have been particularly
easy, and would have been in effect a stabilizing innovation. It is thus at least
possible that the rise of the plural genitive-accusative was a response not only
to nominative-accusative syncretism but also to the far more general fluidity
of the plural paradigms. As already noted, and as works such as Unbegaun
(1935) attest, there is ample evidence both of fluidity and of the use of

referential criteria such as either animacy or personal reference to help organize the changes underway.

In the preceding paragraphs, we have seen that Old Russian noun classification was highly unstable, and that what remained of Indoeuropean declension classes at the beginning of the Old Russian period deteriorated extensively in the succeeding four to five centuries. Clearly, viewed strictly as a system of classification, Old Russian declensional patterns suffered from a lack of any perceptible organizing principles. In this situation, gender provided a stable basis for reorganization, and a sex-based gender system such as the one Old Russian had inherited from Indoeuropean provided a natural context for the development of the morphological expression of distinctions between sexual and asexual beings — animate vs. inanimate, or human vs. nonhuman. Generally, the expected relation between animacy and sex gender is one in which the latter is subordinate to the former, since sex distinctions are obviously impossible for asexual (inanimate) beings (see Hjelmslev 1956/1959); however, these relations were re-ranked, apparently because of the chronological priority of sex gender in Slavic and the specific context of Old Russian declension (see Jakobson 1960/1971).

Thus, the noun (and adjective) genitive-accusative expanded in Old Russian during a period of massive restructuring of the whole inflexional system, when gender was becoming the basis of noun classification. During this restructuring, animacy and/or human reference affected the progress of change in various ways, as noted above, and provided a clear and natural referential articulation of the increasingly important gender system. Consequently, throughout its history, genitive-accusative syncretism in animate or personal nouns has served as a mode of noun classification, even though the precise limits of the syncretism itself were not stabilized until the early modern period.

3. Personal to animate: the chronology of the noun genitive-accusative.

In the preceding sections, we have examined the relation of nominal genitive-accusative syncretism to other phenomena of Old Russian declension — pronominal genitive-accusative syncretism, on the one hand, and, on the other, changes in Old Russian noun inflexion outside the accusative case. In the remainder of this chapter, we will examine more closely the chronology of the noun genitive-accusative itself and its main two extensions: from singular to plural and from human-referential nouns to all nouns referring to living beings. In general, these two extensions of the genitive-accusative were underway at the same time, although the extension to the plural of human nouns was completed by the beginning of the 17th century, whereas the plural animal-noun genitive-accusative was only beginning to appear at that time

(Kedajtene 1961:187). Moreover, in 15th-century writing, the masculine plural genitive-accusative was widespread for nouns of human reference, whereas even the singular of the genitive-accusative for animal nouns was still unusual.

It is generally agreed that the plural human-referential genitive-accusative is first attested in the 14th century; a few attempts to find earlier attestations seem to be based either on unusually early dating of the texts in which the examples are found, or involve apparent misinterpretations: for example, the accusative *tьxъ* found in the Smolensk treaty of 1229, cited in Chapter Three as example (3), is adduced by Dietze (1973:267) as an early example of animacy marking, whereas the early use of the genitive-accusative of demonstrative pronouns seems not to have been conditioned by human or animate reference, or, for that matter, by number (see Chapter Three, §1). Examples of genitive-accusative forms of *inyi* 'some', *samъ* '(one)self' and other pronouns are widespread in the literature on the animate genitive-accusative, and are certainly attested from before the 14th century, but the same objection applies here as well. In addition, genitive forms apparently conditioned by negation have also been treated as early genitive-accusatives (thus, according to Dietze, 1973:267, Kedajtene, in a work unavailable to me).[2]

In the 14th century, on the other hand, attestations are fairly widespread, both in charters and in chronicle texts, as well as in religious writing. A few examples follow:

(1) *sozva boljarъ i kyjanъ*
     'called together the boyars and the Kievans' (Lavr. Ms., 87d 14)
(2) *požalovalъ esmь sokolnikovъ pečerskixъ*
     'I have awarded the Pečerskij falconers' (writ of Ivan Kalita, copy 14th c., cited from Sobolevskij 1907/1962:200)
(3) *ostavi mertvyxъ pogrebъsti svoja mertveca*
     'leave the dead to bury their dead' (Ev. 1383, 19 ob., cited Sobolevskij 1907/1962:200)

With respect to the last example, it may be noted that adjectives on the whole seem to have been inclined to take the plural genitive-accusative earlier than substantives.

According to Kedajtene (1961), Filin (1972:402–403), and others, there is apparent even in the 14th century a clear split between northern and southern texts with respect to the plural genitive-accusative, and this split is reflected in the later histories of Russian and Ukrainian, which was much slower to implement the plural genitive-accusative and retains a nongenitive accusative plural form even for personal nouns in some contemporary folkloric expressions. In Russian, on the other hand, the plural genitive-accusative for masculine human-referential nouns was normal by the 15th century, although

accusatives governed by prepositions were still generally not syncretic with the
genitive even in Unbegaun's corpus from the first half of the 16th century
(Unbegaun 1935:225–236). In addition, there were some other restrictions
apparently still operative in the 16th century, such as the tendency, noted by
Unbegaun, for accusatives modified by possessive pronouns to take the
genitive-accusative more readily than nouns lacking modifiers; Kedajtene
(1961:186) notes that certain plural nouns, generally with collective meanings,
such as *ljudi* or *gosti*, were particularly resistant to the genitive-accusative. In
the 17th century, the genitive-accusative became generalized for masculine
personal nouns, except for very occasional set phrases and some apparently
collective uses of *deti* and *ljudi*. (Kedajtene 1961:186–187, Cocron 1962:100).
At this time, the genitive-accusative was also extended to feminine plural
nouns of human reference (Cocron 1962:101). As noted, the extension of the
genitive-accusative to masculine plural nouns generally followed the loss of a
distinct masculine nominative plural form, but preceded the loss of gender in
the plural oblique cases.

At the same time as the masculine genitive-accusative was extending into
the plural, it was also being expanded in the singular, to include masculine
nouns referring to animals. The conditions under which animal nouns could
occur in the genitive-accusative are essentially the same as for the genitive-
accusative in other instances, but the usage is narrower. As has been noted
above (see especially Chapter Two, §2), the early genitive-accusative is not
always distinct from genitive forms that are syntactically conditioned; for
example, the verbs *jati, viděti,* and *poběditi* are all reported as taking the
genitive as well as the accusative in Old Church Slavonic (Xodova 1963:
56–65), but their genitive rection in my corpus is restricted to the 11th-century
gospel texts; on the other hand, the early examples of animal-noun genitive-
accusatives (if this is what they are) occur disproportionately often as objects
of these verbs. Thus, for example, the 13th-century Life of Savva contains the
following example:

(4)   *i čjudьnago togo lьva viděvь*
      'and seeing that wondrous lion'. (Savva, 107, 13–14)

Here, the presence of the modifiers as well as government by a participle
rather than by a personal verb form would tend to favor the appearance of a
genitive-accusative, and the genitive-accusative for the demonstrative *togo* is
completely normal; thus, if the animal-noun genitive-accusative is even marginally possible for this text, then example (4) offers the ideal environment for it.
At the same time, genitive rection for the verb *viděti* cannot be completely
excluded, although it does not occur elsewhere in this text, where *viděti* with

the accusative is well attested. Although the text is relatively early for animal-noun genitive-accusatives, other examples from the 13th century are known, namely the following two (cited from Kuznecov 1965:223):

(5) *iže kamenь vьrgъ na pъsa*
'he who has cast a stone at a dog' (Rjazan' kormčaja, 1284)
(6) *vergъšago kamenь na psa*
'having cast a stone at a dog'. (Pand. Nikon, 1296)

To make matters worse, many of the verbs whose rection is unclear are illustrated by Xodova and others with animal-noun direct objects, and some inanimate nouns that occur as genitive-form objects in Old Church Slavonic and early Old Russian can be argued to have been treated as personifications — for example, *mirъ* 'world, treaty, peace' — a possibility that yet further reduces the number of really clear examples. The same difficulties apply to two forms occasionally cited as examples of animal genitive-accusatives from the Laurentian Chronicle:

(7) *ön že ... ja vorona*
'and he ... caught the raven' (66a 01–03)
(8) *i vidě ösla stojašča na igumeni městě*
'and he saw an ass standing in the abbot's place'. (64d02–03)

Neither of the verbs governing the genitive forms above is attested with genitive case rection in the Laurentian Manuscript, or, for that matter, else-where in original 14th-century Old Russian texts; the difficulty is that neither of the examples above is entirely original 14th-century Old Russian, since both are from narratives of the lives of saints, which must have been composed by people who were familiar with the genitive rection of these verbs in the gospel texts. Again, the usual analysis of these examples, according to which the genitive forms are genitive-accusatives, cannot be rejected, since animal-noun genitive-accusatives do occur, albeit rarely, in the same manuscript, under an earlier chronological heading (see below). It is quite possible that the genitive forms in the examples cited above represented genitive rection for the original author of the passages in question, but genitive-accusatives for later copyists. In any event, the situation here is reminiscent of the one noted in Chapter Two with respect to early occurrences of the anaphoric masculine singular genitive-accusative *ego*: the genitive-accusative is very often indistinguishable from a genitive-case object, and the earliest instances of forms interpretable as genitive-accusatives are characteristic of Slavonic texts. The preponderance of Slavonic examples need be nothing more than a trivial result of the general preponderance of Slavonic texts as a whole for the period in question; how-ever, there is, at the very least, no evidence that the early animal-noun genitive-accusatives were colloquial innovations either in Old Russian as a whole or in chronicle texts in particular.

To continue with the attestations found in the Laurentian Manuscript, we may note the following passage, beginning at leaf 42 c, line 32:

(9) *nětu li byka byka* [sic] *velika i silna i nalězoša bykъ velikъ i silenъ i povelě razdražditi byka vozložiša na nь želěza goręča i byka pustiša i poběže bykъ mimo i i poxvati byka rukoju za bokъ ... vypustiša pečenězi mužь svoi*
'Isn't there a bull? A big strong bull? And they found a bull (acc.) big and strong and he ordered that they tease the bull (gen.-acc.?) and they laid hot irons to it (acc.) and they released the bull (gen.-acc.?) and the bull ran past him (acc.) and he seized the bull (gen.-acc.?) by the side, with his hand ... the Pečenegs released their man (acc.)'

As is shown by the appearance of the nominative-accusative *mužь svoi* 'their man' at the end of the passage, even human-referential nouns had not yet generalized the singular genitive-accusative in this text, and the anaphoric pronouns referring to people and animals are, as we would expect, in the nongenitive accusative form. The first occurrence of *byka* is clearly a genitive, conditioned by negation, and the first direct-object occurrence of the same word is unambiguously accusative. Nothing here would lead us to expect particularly innovative use of the genitive-accusative. There are, however, three object occurrences of *byka*, governed by (*povelě*) *razdražditi, pustiša,* and *poxvati* respectively. Can these occurrences of *byka* be treated as genitive-case forms?

Lexically, all these verbs seem to govern the accusative case, although *poxvatiti* is not clearly attested in the Laurentian Manuscript and would seem to be an excellent candidate for taking a partitive object. *Pustiti*, on the other hand, occurs with an accusative object elsewhere in the manuscript, does not occur there with a genitive-case object, and even occurs in prefixed form with an accusative object, in the passage cited above. Thus, *byka* is very likely a genitive-accusative in at least the first two of the three occurrences under consideration. In one of the two occurrences, the genitive-accusative is governed by a personal verb form, and in the other instance by an infinitive; we have already noted that there is a strong positive correlation between early genitive-accusatives and nonpersonal verb government (see Chapter Two). Moreover, the apparent genitive-accusatives are definite, whereas the nominative-accusative direct-object *bykъ* is indefinite; the correlation of the genitive-accusative with definiteness has also been noted above (see also Chapter Five and Klenin 1980b). Thus, example (9) above illustrates fairly widespread tendencies in early occurrences of the genitive-accusative, not only among animal nouns but also in other classes of words: the distinction between genitive-accusatives and genitive objects is unclear, and the typical genitive-accusative appears with definite reference, governed by a nonpersonal verb form.

At least one other example of an animal-noun genitive-accusative in the Laurentian Manuscript has been mentioned in the literature (Nekrasov 1905:54); however, this example is spurious, since the genitive form *konę* 'horse' is clearly conditioned by negation:

(10) *i ne bęše lъzě konę napoiti na lybedi*
      'and it was not possible to water a horse on the Lybeď.' (20a 18–19)

There are no animal-noun genitive-accusatives in the other 14th-century chronicle text, the Synod copy of the First Novgorod Chronicle (see Dietze 1973:270–271). There are two possible examples in birchbark letters of the 14th century, No. 266 (written between 1369 and 1382) and No. 124 (written between 1396 and 1409). Neither example is clear; in fact, No. 124 as a whole is unclear, and the putative genitive-accusative *borana*, according to Arcixovskij (Arcixovskij and Borkovskij 1958c: 58–59), means not 'sheep' but 'fishing tackle', a meaning, as Arcixovskij observes, that is otherwise unknown and which, as Borkovskij notes (Arcixovskij and Borkovskij 1958a:116), even if it is correct, does little to enhance our understanding of the text, the more so since *boranъ* in the meaning of 'fishing tackle' is even less likely to occur in the genitive-accusative than is *boranъ* if it means 'sheep'. The text follows, cited in its entirety but without translation, as a conundrum for the reader:

(11) *prišlite mi paroboko borana ili udu mně sę ne možet sę a lodku dai pavlu sobolecevu izonama*
      (cited from Arcixovskij and Borkovskij 1958a:58)

Birchbark 266 reads as follows (cited from Arcixovskij and Borkovskij 1963:94)

(12) *rešь. veli maksmcju. brati. da syplь. sъbi. v klitь. a ir ... poimi. mojego calca. kormi. ježe. dnь. ovsъmъ. a tobi pogixa ... ovъ. poimi. kone. korilesky a čto obilie ... mitrovi.*

The groups of three dots are lacunae noted by the editors, who do not supply a complete translation, presumably because the fragmentary nature of the text does not support one. A rough gloss might be something on the order of: 'Tell Maximec to take ... Spread it in your storeroom ... take my sick horse, feed it with oats daily ... take the Karelian horses and as for the grain ...' The form *calca* is taken by the editors to show cokanie, from a form derived from *čalъ* 'sick'. Although, owing to the nature of the document, its interpretation is unclear, the use of *calca* as an early genitive-accusative is not far-fetched. The governing verb is one of those discussed in Chapter Two, as tending to take genitive-accusatives that are marginally interpretable as genitive objects; moreover, the imperative is more likely than present indicative verb forms to take the genitive-accusative (see Chapter Five). The fact that the object itself is definite and is modified by the possessive pronoun also tends to make it a good candidate for the choice of the genitive-accusative (see Chapter Five). Thus, this putative example of a genitive-accusative fits the criteria that were described above as favoring the appearance of early genitive-accusatives in other word classes.

The examples listed above are the only possible animal genitive-accusatives in my corpus from before 1400. At least one additional example is cited by Kedajtene (see footnote 2); Dietze (1973:270) cites from Kedajtene the following example, from a document of 1270:

(13)   *uljubilъ esi edinogo konja*
       'you have selected a certain horse'

Dietze suggests that the prefixed form of the verb could have conditioned genitive government, but, if so, this is not usual with this verb, and I know of no other instances. Again, the appearance of the genitive-accusative at this early date is, of course, unexpected, but the environment in which it appears is one that is known to favor the appearance of the genitive-accusative, because of the presence of the modifier.

There are several well-known examples from the early 16th century, although, according to Unbegaun (1935:227), they are highly exceptional. Unbegaun himself adduces only a single such example, cited from Karpov (1884:605):

(14)   *čtoby namъ kъ tobě poslati pesъ borzoj da sobaku podsokolьju da krečetъ i my kъ tobě pesъ borzoj i sobaku podsokolьju i krečeta poslali.*
       'that we should send you a borzoi dog and a falconing dog and a gyrfalcon; and we sent you the borzoi dog and the falconing dog and the gyrfalcon (gen.-acc.)'.

As in the previous example, the genitive-accusative appears in a favorable environment, since the word's reference is definite (cf. the examples of *byka* from the Laurentian Manuscript above). Unbegaun's example is from 1521, as is the following one, provided by Borkovskij (1949:374):

(15)   *a kotoroj novogorodecъ konь kupitъ vъ Mesterove drьžave … a privedetъ togo konja*
       'and if any Novgorodian buys a horse in the Master's jurisdiction … and brings that horse (gen.-acc.)'

Here, the reference of the genitive-accusative word is definite, and is modified by a demonstrative pronoun (cf. *edinogo* in example (13) above). Moreover, as we saw in Chapter Three, the demonstratives themselves take the genitive-accusative form even in our earliest texts, regardless of animate or human reference or other restrictions. Thus, the appearance of the noun genitive-accusative may have been favored by its proximity to a demonstrative modifier that normally would have appeared in the genitive-accusative if no noun head had been present. Of course, the influence could have worked the other way; for example, in the plural, where the genitive-accusative of animal nouns was completely excluded before the 17th century, we find nominative-accusative demonstratives:

(16) *ty, knęžo, tye kone öbizrelъ*
      'you, Prince, examined those horses'.

(This example is from the same text as (13) above, which immediately follows it in the original document.) Such interaction of elements has often been noted with respect to the genitive-accusative of human-referential masculine singular nouns in early Old Russian texts. Thus, for example, proper names nearly always appeared in the genitive-accusative, but the noun *synъ* 'son' tended not to; when a proper noun appeared in apposition with the noun *synъ*, the results were usually to use the genitive-accusative, less commonly to use the nominative-accusative, and only seldom to combine the two possibilities. The conditions favoring the appearance of the genitive-accusative are discussed more fully in Chapter Five.

Additional examples of early genitive-accusatives of animal nouns, also in the singular, are adduced by Cocron (1962:98–99), who points out that all the occurrences of *žerebec* 'stallion, colt' in the accusative are genitive-accusative in the narrative of Afanasij Nikitin (as recorded in the Troickij Manuscript, copied no later than the early 16th century). There are altogether four examples of genitive-accusative *žerebca*, of which three are definite. The fourth example, which appears below, has no clear motivation:

(17) *i jazъ grěšnyj privezlъ žerebьca v Yndějskuju zemlju*
      'and I, sinner, brought a stallion to the Indian land'. (Nikitin, 1958, leaf 373)

In addition to the four occurrences of *žerebca*, we also find the following example in the same narrative:

(18) *Indějane že vola zovutь otcemъ*
      'the Indians call the bullock their father'. (Nikitin, 379)

The manuscript contains no examples of nongenitive accusative animal nouns in the singular, although only the nongenitive accusative occurs in the plural. In view of the small number of even likely, if unclear, examples from this period, the occurrence of five animal-noun genitive-accusatives in just this one text is a striking anomaly. Such 'bunching' of examples, in this text or in one small part of the Laurentian manuscript, lends support to Cocron's opinion that there may have been considerable variation in genitive-accusative usage according to genres, and in some kinds of writing there may have been much freer use of the genitive-accusative of masculine singular animal nouns than would appear from even a large corpus that did not include sufficiently varied material. Since, on the other hand, there is a dearth of colloquial texts, as well as of texts that happen to deal, like Afanasij Nikitin's narrative, with the transport of horses, it is not possible easily to pursue this possibility.

In any event, all animal-noun genitive-accusatives from before the 17th century are masculine singular nouns; moreover, they seem to have been rare and occurred mainly in textual environments otherwise known to have strongly favored the genitive-accusative. In the 17th century, the situation changes: the genitive-accusative becomes the normal accusative form for masculine singular animal nouns, and is also attested in the plural. There is variation in plural usage throughout the 17th century. In general, Cocron finds the genitive-accusative normal for plural animal nouns, whereas the nominative-accusative tends to be restricted — occurring under prepositional government, for example. However, the nominative-accusative plural, although restricted, was clearly more widespread than the nominative-accusative singular, which seems to have occurred only in certain cliches, or with certain nouns, particularly *конь* 'horse', which has been peculiarly resistant to the genitive-accusative. Pennington (1980:313), discussing Kotošixin's *O Rossii v carstvovanie Alekseja Mixajloviča*, considers the plural genitive-accusative exceptional, and notes that some forms taken by Cocron to be genitive-accusatives are more correctly interpreted as genitive objects. The disputed examples will not be treated here, since they are discussed in full by Pennington. To some extent at least, it is likely that the difference between Cocron's and Pennington's interpretations is a function of the different texts they are examining. Again, Cocron notes differences in usage depending on the kind of text, apparently deliberate archaization of language, and so on. He also notes a nominative-accusative and a genitive-accusative plural of the same word occurring nearly side-by-side in the comedy *Amfitrion: Zaderži svoix konej* 'Hold your horses (gen.-acc.)' vs. *Zaderži svoi koni*. The general picture of flux and expansion of the plural animal-noun genitive-accusative remains the same in any event. Clearly, this was the last class of genitive-accusatives to be stabilized, and, dialectally, a nominative-accusative apparently has been recorded even in modern North Russian dialects at least for the noun *koni*. (It can be disputed whether the recorded forms represent a nominative-accusative or a nominative object; in favor of the former interpretation is the fact that the disputed form does occur as the object of a preposition, but the rarity of such data casts some doubt on their reliability. For further discussion, see Kuz'mina-Nemčenko 1964:168.) As noted above, Russian and Ukrainian have differed from the 14th century with respect to animal-noun genitive-accusatives, and the plural nominative-accusative can still be found in Modern Ukrainian dialects.

It is thus clear that the genitive-accusative in Old Russian nouns was referentially more narrowly restricted than in Modern Russian; moreover, the referential restrictions on the genitive-accusative were relaxed in the singular before they were relaxed in the plural, and earliest in contexts that strongly favored the appearance of the genitive-accusative as a whole. Such a weakening of referential conditions to include not only animal nouns but also some inanimates has occurred throughout Slavic, but always in the singular only. In the next chapter, we will explore the conditions on the genitive-accusative more fully.

NOTES

1. It has occasionally been suggested, most notably by Sørensen (1959), that the loss of the old instrumental in -*y* was motivated by its formal identity with the accusative and nominative plural in the same words — yet another possible connection between genitive-accusative syncretism and other ongoing changes in the plural declension. See, however, Pennington 1980:236.

2. E. I. Kedajtene, *Razvitie form roditel'nogo-vinitel'nogo padeža i upotreblenie staryx form vinitel'nogo ot nazvanij lic i oduševlennyx predmetov v drevnerusskom jazyke (na materiale pamjatnikov 12–14 vv.)*, Mokslo darbai, Vilniaus Valstybinis V. Kapsuko vardo universitetas, Istorijos-filologijos mokslų serija, t. 3, 1957, page 145 ff. Work cited in Dietze 1973:264.

PART TWO

Chapter Five. Conditions on the Genitive-Accusative: Correlations with Case Marking.

In each of the preceding three chapters, we examined one or another attested stage in the history of the Russian genitive-accusative. The remaining two chapters will offer a less strictly diachronic perspective on the genitive-accusative, but instead will focus on more general aspects of its correlation with case (Chapter Five) and gender (Chapter Six).

I have argued above in favor of Meillet's analysis of the genitive-accusative as a true (syntactic) accusative form, syncretic with the genitive, instead of being, at least in its premodern stages, a syntactic genitive. This analysis, of course, is incompatible with the view that the genitive-accusative in Modern Russian is a genitive case form, as suggested by Nekrasov (1905) and van Schooneveld (1977). As discussed by Meillet with respect to Old Church Slavonic, the differences between the genitive-accusative and syntactic genitive case forms are striking: the genitive-accusative can occur conjoined with accusatives but not with genitives, and genitive-accusative modifiers can occur with non-genitive accusative head nouns, but not with nonsyncretic genitives. In addition, the genitive-accusative occurs in any environment in which accusatives are permitted, but is morphologically restricted to just certain declension classes; syntactic genitive case forms, on the contrary, can appear only in syntactic conditions that trigger the genitive case, and are not morphologically restricted.

However, the fact that genitive-accusatives are distinct from genitive case forms does not invalidate the relation between the two. Meillet, as we have seen, viewed this relation as essentially fortuitous, since he incorrectly argued for the original accusative status of the first genitive-accusatives, which then served as the analogical model for later extensions. Thomson and later scholars developing his approach have also tended to view the genitive-accusative as an analogical development, the model for which they generally saw as the partitive genitive or the genitive of negation. According to this school of thought, the genitive-accusative was implemented as an analogical syntactic rule, formulated in response to communicative needs; eventually, however, the syntactic conditions on the genitive-accusative were lost, and the rule was morphologized. In the preceding discussion, I have suggested an alternative hypothesis — that the genitive-accusative represents, historically, a morphological reanalysis of genitive case objects, in environments where genitive rection was being lost. The genitives reanalyzed in this way seem to have been of virtually all types, judging both from the early examples of genitive-accusatives and from the ultimate loss in Russian of all kinds of genitive verbal rection.

The difference between my hypothesis and earlier ones can be reduced to the following main points. First, I have found no evidence at all that the genitive-accusative was ever a syntactic phenomenon, as distinct from the morphological phenomenon that it now is. Correspondingly, there is no process of morphologization internal to the history of the genitive-accusative. A process of morphologization (or morphological reanalysis) did occur, but only at the threshold of the implementation of the genitive-accusative, and it marks precisely the point at which the genitive-accusative arose out of the moribund genitive-case objects that gave rise to it.

Second, there is no need to posit any innovation of the genitive-accusative independent of the loss of genitive-case direct objects in Russian. It must be stressed that there was no period in the history of Russian (or of Slavic) characterized either by stable genitive-case verbal rection or by absence of the genitive-accusative. Although the early appearance of the genitive-accusative is well known, apparently the early weakness of genitive verbal rection is less so. For example, the genitive of negation is widely reported to have been completely obligatory and stable through the mid-19th century; however, Karskij (1929/1962) points to several interesting examples of the use of accusative for expected genitive under negation in the Primary Chronicle, and his examples suggest that these early accusatives are actually of sorts that regularly occur as accusatives under negation in modern Russian, according to Timberlake (1975) and sources cited therein. In view of this situation, and in view of the existence of large quantities of ambiguous data, such as that discussed in Chapter Two, we may reasonably suggest that the deterioration and ultimate loss of genitive verbal rection in Russian was to a very great extent actually the same event as the rise of the genitive-accusative. What happened to the genitive objects that were lost is that they were morphologically reanalyzed as genitive-accusative; the source of the genitive-accusative was the morphological reanalysis of genitive objects. This interpretation is not actually incompatible with a functionalist analysis of the genitive-accusative, such as Thomson presents; the interpretation given here, however, does entail a very different evaluation of the materials adduced by Thomson, and provides a structural description of the rise of the genitive-accusative that is independent of communicative functionality in the sense of Thomson's proposal. In other words, Thomson's hypothesis with regard to the functionality of the genitive-accusative cannot be proven with the arguments he provides (see Chapter One for discussion); moreover, even if his views are correct in the most general terms (that is, if the rise of the genitive-accusative did actually contribute to distinguishing subject from object), this still does not motivate any particular analysis of how the change actually occurred.

The idea that the genitive-accusative represents a reanalysis of genitive-case objects is not new, and has been suggested by Kuryłowicz (1962) and, indirectly, Sommer (1916). However, previous studies, even those recognizing genitive-case objects as a source for the genitive-accusative, have never actually identified the incipient genitive-accusative with the declining genitive objects. What I would like to put before the reader here is actually what may be thought of as the radical extension of an interpretation in which the genitive-accusative is said to have arisen by means of morphological reanalysis. In this "radical" view, the ambiguous genitive-form objects, such as those discussed in detail in Chapters Two and Four, are interpretable only retrospectively, in the light of the ultimate history of such constructions. This history consists precisely in the replacement of genitive objects with genitive-accusatives in the grammar of Russian; therefore, as soon as constructions with genitive-form objects are structurally ambiguous, this ambiguity must be the result of the relevant historical change having already got under way. Therefore, such data must be symptomatic precisely of the loss of the old genitives. By definition, the structurally ambiguous data can be analyzed as genitive-accusative, because the genitive-accusative must already be functioning in the grammar for the marginal examples to have arisen at all. In the analysis I am proposing directly below, the genitive-accusative can be viewed as having fed on the remains of *all* the old genitive object rules, without having had any particular relation to any one of them. More crudely, the genitive-accusative actually *was* what became of the old genitive objects — an historical model that can be called You Are What You Eat.

It is also important that, as we have seen, the genitive-accusative did not arise out of genitive-case forms and thereafter develop independently. On the contrary, the genitive-accusative at every stage of its expansion in Old Russian re-established its early connection with genitive case objects. This recurrent association of the genitive-accusative with genitive case objects takes two rather different forms.

First, at every stage in its implementation, the genitive-accusative appeared first in direct-object position, and only later in prepositional phrases. As noted above, this tendency has been considered evidence of the original motivation of the genitive-accusative as an object-marking rule; however, its recurrence at different stages of the genitive-accusative suggests rather that reanalysis of syntactic genitive case forms provided the mechanism for implementing the genitive-accusative, regardless of original motivation. Thus, for example, the motivation for the extension of the genitive-accusative to masculine noun plurals is likely to have been at least partly a tendency to reunite the plural paradigm with its corresponding singular; this motivation cannot have played any role at all in the singular, and yet the manner of the extension of the genitive-accusative was essentially the same. Consequently, motivation need not be clearly reflected in a rule's mode of implementation.

The second type of recurrent association between the several stages of the genitive-accusative and the genitive case is of a different kind, involving not just a single syntactic condition, such as the direct-object condition just mentioned, but rather a whole group of conditions of the most varied sort — all the conditions, in fact, noted in Chapters Two through Four and summarized for ease of reference in Table (5–1).

Table 5–1

Summary of Conditions on the Genitive-Accusative at Various Stages of Its Implementation.

FACTOR FAVORING THE GENITIVE-ACCUSATIVE	FORM CLASSES AFFECTED	CHAPTER DISCUSSED
— OBJECT NOUN PHRASE		
Status as:		
Demonstrative Pronoun		III
Emphatic Pronoun		III
kogo		III
Declension Class:		
o-, jo-stems	Nouns	IV
Nom.-Acc. Syncretism	All	I, II, III, IV
Gender:		
Masculine	Anaphoric Pronouns	II
Number:		
Singular	All but Personal Pronouns	II, IV
Plural	Personal Pronouns	III
Reference:		
Human (Animate)	Nouns	IV
Proper	Nouns	IV
Definite	Nouns	IV
Preposed/Contrastive	Personal Pronouns	III
Modification	Nouns	IV
— GOVERNING FORM		
Direct-Object Position	All	I
Verb or Predicate Semantics	All	II – IV
Non-Personal Verb Form	All	II
— STYLE		
Colloquial	Nouns (?)	IV
Slavonic	All (?)	II, III, IV

In the table, the relevant factors are grouped according to whether they are conditions depending primarily on features of the object noun phrase or its elements, or are features of the governing (verb or prepositional) form or are related to more general stylistic choices. The rubrics in the table are suggestive only, since detailed discussion is provided in earlier chapters, as indicated in the table. The correlation of factors with form classes (the second column in the table) takes note only of form classes within which the progress of the genitive-accusative can be adequately described only if the given factor is taken into account; thus, for example, we saw in Chapters Two and Four that animate or human reference is not a factor ordering the implementation of the genitive-accusative in pronouns, although the predominantly human reference of pronouns may well have affected their general sensitivity to the genitive-accusative. Thus, in Table 5–1 Human (or Animate) reference is listed as a factor affecting the noun genitive-accusative, but not the pronoun genitive-accusative. The conditions listed in Table 5–1 are obviously heterogeneous: some are much more general than others in their range of application, and they include lexical and stylistic factors as well as both syntactic and morphological ones. Nevertheless, all the conditions listed share an important characteristic: they are relevant to the history not only of the genitive-accusative but also of genitive case-marking rules such as the genitive of negation or the partitive genitive.

Of peculiar interest here is the overlap between the conditions noted above and the set of conditions known as 'individuation' restrictions on the Modern Russian genitive of negation rule. As is well known, Modern Russian retains a rule permitting genitive case marking on direct objects of negated verbs, but this rule is being lost, and there are a number of conditions blocking genitive case marking in such constructions. One major generalization about the choice of the genitive or the accusative is that the accusative is preferred insofar as the direct object is individuated — that is to say, is definite or specific in reference, preposed or contrastively stressed, modified, singular in number, referentially animate, or proper. (A complete description of individuation in the genitive of negation is found in Timberlake 1975, where the notion is first proposed. A more detailed application of the relation of individuation features to the genitive-accusative is found in Klenin 1980b). These features of direct objects, then, are relevant to the choice of accusative or genitive case form not only when the choice is on the level of inflexional morphology, as in the genitive-accusative, but also when it reflects a choice between two distinct cases, as in the genitive of negation rule. Moreover, the syntactic relevance of individuation is not restricted to the genitive of negation, but applies also to the partitive genitive.

Thus, individuation is apparently relevant to the semantics associated with genitive forms, regardless of the grammatical status or source of the genitive. However, the effect of individuation is not the same in the genitive-accusative as it is in the operation of the syntactic genitive case marking rules, since individuation generally promotes the appearance of an *accusative* in the syntactic rules, whereas it generally promotes the appearance of the *genitive*-syncretic accusative case form. For example, definite direct objects tend not to be marked as genitives under the genitive of negation rule, but definite direct objects were among the earliest accusatives to take the genitive-accusative, for example among animal nouns, as discussed in Chapter Four. The same is true for all the other individuation features: they favor the appearance of syntactically conditioned accusatives, but of morphological genitives.

In addition to the individuation features, other conditions on the genitive-accusative are also known to be relevant to the genitive of negation, and, again, the influence of these conditions is generally opposite in the two different types of rule. For example, any predicate other than a simple declarative one with a personal verb form in the imperfective aspect is likely not to permit the genitive of negation — secondary complements, perfective aspect, infinitive mood, and so on. These conditions, as we have seen, are historically the ones most likely to trigger the genitive-accusative. Similarly, accusatives other than direct objects may be genitive-marked under negation, but are more likely to have accusative case marking — again the opposite of the genitive-accusative rule. There are only two clear exceptions to the general rule that the conditions on the genitive of negation are inverted when applied to the genitive-accusative — namely, the exemption of second-declension *a*-stems from genitive case marking and the general tendency of certain individual verbs, such as verbs of perception, to favor the use of the genitive. In addition to the inversion of certain conditions on the genitive of negation, the conditions may be differently ranked when applied to the genitive-accusative; for example, animacy is of unique importance for the genitive-accusative of nouns, whereas it is not nearly so important for the operation of the genitive of negation rule. Thus, the conditions shared by the genitive-accusative and the genitive of negation rules may have a completely different status in one rule as compared with the other, as is shown by the conditions being either inverted or re-ranked. There are, however, no known conditions on the genitive of negation that are completely irrelevant to the history of the genitive-accusative.

Many of the conditions mentioned above, both the so-called individuation features of the direct object and the features such as verbal aspect that are presumably verbal or predicative features, are generally correlated not only with Russian genitive-object marking rules but also with transitivity and object-marking constructions in many other languages as well (see Hopper-Thompson 1980). In terms of transitivity in general, the Russian genitive-object marking rules such as the genitive of negation apparently reflect reduced levels of transitivity by means of genitive case marking, as compared with the more fully transitive constructions with accusative case objects, with which the genitive object marking alternates. In terms of a Jakobsonian approach to case marking, the use of the genitive case correponds to the relatively limited participation of the object in the speech event — that is, the genitive-marked object is less fully a semantic object, or patient, than is the accusative direct object. Since the genitive-accusative historically referred to these same conditions, it too was in effect an object-marking rule, according to which the genitive-accusative was preferentially used in the most fully transitive construction. Thus, the genitive-accusative at least ephemerally functioned as an object marking rule clearly akin to syntactic rules of genitive case marking. The nature of the relation, however, is complicated, since the output of the genitive-accusative rule was a genitive form for highly transitive objects, whereas the genitive usually marks, and marked, reduced transitivity.

This apparent contradiction can, however, be explained. First, we may object to the assumption that the genitive-case form as such is, or was, a marker of reduced transitivity. Instead, we might propose that the genitive case form has no very particular meaning, but simply marks those direct objects that deviate in one or another way from the expected transitive relation, without having the specific semantic characteristics of, say, dative or instrumental objects. That is, the genitive case form indicates, roughly, abnormal transitivity, whether plus or minus. (This, of course, must be kept distinct from the question of a general meaning for the genitive case, which, as we have seen, is not represented by the genitive-accusative.) The distribution of genitive forms can be compared in this respect with the distribution of other case forms, notably the instrumental. The instrumental case in Russian marks real instruments, used by agents in performing actions, as well as forces of nature responsible for events that are presented as outside human control; that is, the instrumental marks discourse participants in roles that typically cannot be taken by human-referential noun phrases. At the same time, the other characteristic use of the instrumental case is as a comitative case, where the noun phrase in the instrumental is nearly always human (or at least animate), and may occur in virtually any sentence role or function, including that of the subject. Thus, the Russian instrumental has two characteristic roles, each with a strong correlation with human referentiality of noun phrases — but the correlation is reversed in the two instances.

In a different sort of example, modern Ukrainian has developed dative-locative syncretism for masculine animate nouns in the singular. The dative is one of the most frequent cases in which human-referential nouns appear, whereas the locative is the least frequent. Thus, a single form marks both the most and least typical cases of human-referential nouns.

Thus, case forms not only can come to mark noun phrases in a broad range of functions, but can also mark two restricted ranges at opposite extremes of a single scale — in these instances, a scale of human/animate/inanimate referentiality. The lack of formal differentiation between the two uses of each form presents no interpretational problems, particularly since both Ukrainian and Russian make extensive use of prepositions as well as case endings to mark synactic and semantic status. In the examples introduced above, the human/inanimate referentiality of given noun phrases makes them more or less desirable or likely candidates for particular semantic roles in sentences — as instruments or as accompanying persons, as experiencers of psychological states or as places. The semantic roles themselves, however, cannot be fully defined according to the inherent semantics of the lexical items that can fill them, but instead have fairly clear meanings of their own; these meanings, in turn, have been only partly grammaticalized in the Russian or Ukrainian case systems. That is, whatever meanings are expressed by case endings must be more abstract than such concrete notions as 'experiencer' or 'location', and the notion of 'experiencer' or 'location' can have many expressions other than dative or locative case forms. In describing the duality of expression in genitive object forms, on the contrary, we describe the semantic range of a grammatical property, namely transitivity, for which the referential scale is apparently an essential component. The extent to which a given construction is to be viewed as relatively more or less fully transitive depends in part on the referential properties of the verbal object. For this reason, the question of interpretability or ambiguity is not directly relevant to the marking of transitive objects in the same way as is the marking of instrumental nouns as comitative or as true instrumentals: if a human noun appeared in a true instrumental construction, it would be interpreted as an unusual occurrence of a human instrument, whereas a human-referential direct object cannot be interpreted as other than a direct object, even if the relative strength of the transitive relation is unspecified. In Modern Russian, transitive objects other than those with genitive-accusative syncretism — that is to say all inanimate plural noun phrases and nearly all inanimate singulars — can appear in constructions of reduced transitivity, such as partitive constructions or negated sentences or predicates, where it is possible actually to express the weakening of the transitive relation. On the other hand, some Russian nouns — namely, the ones that have genitive-accusative syncretism — have lost the capacity to express weakened transitivity; the semantics associated with genitive-accusative syncretism, however, assure that these nouns for the most part are unlikely to be weakly transitive objects, because of their animate (human) reference. Thus, the final effect of genitive-accusative syncretism on the expression of transitivity in Russian was to eliminate the possibility of marking inherently highly transitive objects as less than fully transitive. This result came about through the operation of a consistent, long-term historical process, which was always sensitive to transitivity and which always operated preferentially on the most highly transitive objects of each form class implementing the genitive-accusative syncretism rule.

A number of the historic conditions on the genitive-accusative were already known to Thomson, who believed that they provided evidence in support of his view that the first genitive-accusatives were those objects that were most similar to subjects and hence most in need of morphological differentiation from them. As I have indicated in earlier chapters, I consider it unlikely that this interpretation is as fully justified as Thomson thought.

One cause for suspicion lies in the ultimate stabilization of the genitive-accusative. Thomson's analysis requires us to accept the view that the genitive-accusative, having done its original syntactic job, for some reason spread into constructions where its appearance was not motivated, and eventually lost all syntactic value, being retained as a morphological vestige of its former communicative self. Such things do, of course, happen, but it is difficult to explain why, or even how, it should have happened exactly in the way it did here. If the genitive-accusative passed from being a syntactic rule to a morphological phenomenon, why was it not simply generalized in nouns as it was in pronouns, or why was it never left (not only in Russian, but anywhere in Slavic) with even a trace of its original value? Why did it always spread according to morphological classes first, and only secondarily according to syntactic and semantic conditions? Why should the pronoun development have been so different from the noun development, and yet related in the ways it was? What, in particular, was the status of the genitive-accusative during the period when it was being extended into the plural of masculine nouns? At this stage, the genitive-accusative in the singular was already fully (or at least nearly fully) morphologized in the masculine singular, and the plural development, if analogous to anything, must have been at least as analogous to the morphological genitive-accusative already existing in the singular as it was to the genitive of negation, where the mode of analogy is, at least, unclear. Yet in the masculine plural the force of the individuation and other conditions was no less than in the singular; in fact, it is more obvious, because of the fortuitous existence of stronger documentation. Moreover, as we have now seen, the genitive-case object-marking rules were all in the process of being lost; surely rules that were disappearing were undesirable analogical models for the genitive-accusative?

If, on the other hand, the genitive-accusative advanced precisely through morphological reanalysis of syntactic genitive objects, rather than as a result of analogy to them, then the entire, apparently rather complicated, history of the genitive-accusative turns out to have been part of a much more general and well known tendency in the history of Russian. Old Russian had a fairly elaborate system for marking the varying relations of transitive objects to the constructions in which they occurred; this system made extensive use of variable genitive and accusative marking, but it was not restricted to genitive/accusative variation alone, as is shown by the existence of the old nominative direct object found mainly if not entirely in North Russian. In Modern Russian, this system has for the most part disappeared or is disappearing; not only has the nominative object been lost (or reanalyzed) and the various syntactic genitive objects lost or weakened, but the genitive-accusative has effectively removed from the scope of operation of the genitive-marking transitivity rules virtually all animate noun phrases and all the pronouns. We have seen in previous chapters that the various aspects of this syntactic decay fed one on the other, while, at the same time, the inflexional pattern that was emerging served throughout its history as an effective noun classificatory system, whose referential basis was not only clear but also widely utilized in other parts of the grammar. Apparently, but only apparently, paradoxically, the crux of the relation between the genitive-accusative and the syntactic object-marking rules of early and modern Russian is precisely the fact that the genitive-accusative effectively marks a well-defined class of objects without itself being, or ever having been, a part of the system of grammatical (syntactic) rules using case to express syntactic (object) relations.

Thus, we can view the relation between the genitive-accusative and genitive case marking as one of historical complementarity: the genitive-accusative represents a morphological reanalysis of syntactic genitive case objects, which were receding in Old Russian. The genitive-accusative provided an orderly mode of retreat for the syntactic rules, by removing an important class of direct objects from the range of the syntactic rules' operation. Since this class of objects was always at the periphery of the range of the old genitive object marking rules, their removal from that range represented a kind of gradual attrition and weakening of the Old Russian system for expressing transitivity. The genitive-accusative can be viewed as essentially an inverse function of the decline of object-marking rules in Russian.

Although the genitive-accusative thus had a syntactic value, it was itself essentially an inflexional phenomenon. Moreover, the historical syntactic value of the genitive-accusative was never lost, but is reflected in the inaccessibility of most modern Russian animate nouns to genitive and accusative case alternation.

Chapter Six. Animacy: the Genitive-Accusative in Russian Gender

In Chapter Four, we saw that the genitive-accusative had an important role in the history of Russian noun classification, reinforcing the sex-referential system inherited from Indoeuropean. As is well known, this classificatory function of the genitive-accusative is specific to nouns and modifiers; the only pronouns that show a division according to animacy are those that are quasi-adjectival, in that they have an adjectival declension (i.e., the relative pronoun *kotoryj*) or occur as modifiers (the emphatic *sam* or the universal quantifier *vesь*) or both (*ljuboj, vsjakij, každyj,* meaning 'any, every, each'). All pronouns that are not either inflexionally or syntactically quasi-adjectival have generalized the genitive-accusative. On the other hand, in all paradigms in which the genitive-accusative has a classificatory function, it is also a marker of the animate subgender. It will be useful for our discussion below to distinguish the noun-classificatory status of the genitive-accusative from its function in the gender system. As we will use the terms, noun classification is an essentially referential and inflexional notion, whereas gender must be syntactically expressed, through agreement patterns. Noun classification can be based on virtually any set of referential properties (in Russian, sex reference and animacy), and consists of the morphological coding of these properties, which thus form a basis for the organization of inflexional paradigms. Theoretically, noun classification can also be based on nonreferential properties, for example word length or syllable structure, but this type of classification is of no interest for our present purpose and will therefore be ignored here. Gender systems, on the other hand, are a specific elaboration of noun classification, in which classificatory coding is utilized in agreement patterns. My use of terminology throughout this discussion in most respects follows that of Greenberg 1978.

The following description can serve as a rough introduction to the relation between noun classification and gender in Russian. Nouns with nominative singulars in -∅ and belonging to the same declension class as e.g. *stol* 'table', *brat* 'brother', and *professor* 'professor' are in general masculine gender; all the human-referential nouns of this type can be used to refer to males, and until relatively recently all of them normally were so used. Similarly, nouns of the same declension type as *kniga* 'book', *sestra* 'sister', or *učiteľnica* '(woman) teacher' are generally feminine gender, and human-referential nouns belonging to this class usually were nouns used to refer to women. However, the *kniga* class has always included a few nouns that refer only to men (*mužčina* 'man') or at least normally to men (*sud'ja* 'judge'). Such nouns triggered masculine agreement patterns and were therefore classed as masculine in gender.

(Peškovskij, and occasionally others who have tried to take into account the morphological correlations of gender classes have treated such nouns as morphologically feminine, although syntactically masculine. See Peškovskij 1928/1956:93–94.) In addition, the *kniga* type also included some nouns used to refer either to males or to females — *sirota* 'orphan', for example, as well as many nouns of strong emotive or stylistic coloration, such as *plaksa* 'cry-baby'. These nouns are variable with respect to agreement, but always trigger feminine agreement when they are used to refer to females. They are usually called 'common gender' nouns. The other declension classes will be ignored here, because they present no problems of immediate importance for our discussion.

The system that emerges from this survey is quite simple. There is a direct correlation between paradigm type and both sex reference and gender. The agreement patterns triggered by the male-referential *brat* are (except for the genitive-accusative, which is of course restricted to animates) the same as for all the other nouns of its declension class, which by virtue of this association are called 'masculine'. (For a formal characterization of this relation, see Marcus 1962.) Roughly the same can be said of *sestra, kniga*, and the feminine ('a-stem') declension. Where human-referential nouns violate the general pattern, their (syntactic) gender is determined by their sex reference, following the sex referentiality established by the most usual usage of the words. Where the usual usage is not clearly associated with one sex rather than the other, then agreement patterns are variable and depend on the sex of the referent in each separate occurrence. (Nonreferential usage will not be included in this simplified survey.)

The importance of the sex referentiality of nouns like *sudja* or *professor* in determining their agreement is shown by the fact that in the Soviet period, when many formerly all-male professions have been opened to women, there has been increasing variability in the agreement triggered by nouns that are names of professional titles. Although Russian theoretically has the derivational capacity to create feminine equivalents of the traditional titles, along the lines of the well-established pair *učitel* 'teacher' vs. *učitelnica* '(woman) teacher', there has been no strong tendency to use such derivational formations so as to make agreement patters coincide with morphology in an obvious way; if anything, the specifically feminine forms have tended to be restricted to uses in which women members of a profession are contrasted with men, and the meaning of such forms is often pejorative or at least low-prestige. In this respect, Russian clearly differs from some other languages, for example Polish (see Rothstein 1980). Russian, instead, seems at first glance to be re-categorizing nouns, enlarging its original 'common gender' stock to include professional names — see, on this point, Panov 1968:19–41. (Significantly, Polish lacks a 'common gender' of the Russian type, since feminine-declension nouns referring to males actually adopt a 'mixed' masculine/feminine set of inflexional endings; there is thus no class of male-referential nouns inflexionally indistinguishable from feminines. Thus, Polish has no 'common gender' stock that could be enlarged, in the way that Russian does.)

However, this tendency is realized to a different extent in nouns of different declension classes. Nouns of the predominantly feminine -*a* declension, such as *sud'ja*, show little resistance to feminine agreement, but nouns of the predominantly masculine type restrict feminine agreement sharply. In general, to take only one type of restriction, feminine modifier-head agreement occurs with such nouns only in the nominative case; thus, for example, even speakers who freely use constructions such as *molodaja vrač* 'young (f.) doctor (nom.)' nevertheless reject, for example, **vstretit' moloduju vrača* 'to meet the young (f.) doctor (acc.)'. Although the barrier to such usage may conceivably yet be broken down, it nevertheless is very clearly felt now and provides a solid objective basis for saying that *vrač* belongs in a different agreement class from *sud'ja*. Thus, even if *sud'ja* is said to have made the transition to the 'common gender' agreement class, *vrač* cannot be said to have done so, nor is there any reason to suppose that it ever will. The difference in behavior between *vrač* and *sud'ja* is important, and we will return to it later.

Because of the importance of agreement in assigning nouns to genders, agreement patterns are sometimes identified with genders. That is, genders are established as a result of surveying all the different agreement phenomena of the language — in the present instance, modifier-head agreement in all the various cases, subject-predicate concord, and agreement of relative and anaphoric pronouns with their antecedents. Words triggering different sets of inflexional endings in agreeing forms are of different genders, and words triggering the same endings are the same gender; hence, each set of agreeing forms defines a distinct gender. (For detailed discussion of gender discovery procedures, see Revzin 1977:145–151, Karpinskaja 1966, Zaliznjak 1964 and 1967:62–82.) As is, however, well known, this procedure tends to lead to proliferation of genders, and procedures have had to be developed to define the interrelations among the isolated elementary genders defined by the first-stage analysis, for example, the animate and inanimate subgenders of the masculine singular. Nouns that trigger variable agreement patterns of course present special problems; for example, *sirota* 'orphan' can be considered either to represent a special variable-agreement ('common') gender class or to be a pair of masculine and feminine homonyms, synonymous in all respects except sex reference. It should, however, be kept in mind that the different types of agreement (that is, modifier-head agreement, subject-predicate concord of all types, and so on) themselves differ in their stability and therefore in their reliability as indicators of gender. We have already seen that the masculine noun *vrač* 'doctor' can trigger feminine modifier-head agreement, but only in the nominative case. This is actually part of a much more extensive hierarchy: subject-predicate feminine concord with *vrač* is more widespread than is feminine nominative modifier-head agreement, and relative and anaphoric pronouns show feminine agreement probably at least as freely as masculine agreement, if the referent of *vrač* is female. (Agreement hierarchies in Russian are well documented. See, for example, Rothstein 1980, Corbett 1979.) In general, modifier-head agreement is the type of agreement least sensitive to real-world sex reference, when such real-world information conflicts with grammatical coding. For this reason, we can consider modifier-head agreement the phenomenon most basic to syntactic definition of gender. This means that, even if we wish to define gender purely syntactically, on the basis of its effect on agreement patterns, we must still differentiate between those agreement patterns in which gender agreement is fully grammaticalized and stable, and those in which gender agreement is controlled partly by real-world sex reference (ad sensum agreement). This division correponds to the difference between stable and fully grammaticalized noun classification, on the one hand, and, on the other, a more labile type of classification, performed by speakers at each occasion of the use of a noun or noun phrase. That is to say, instability in agreement arises from conflicts and instabilities in noun classification; the part of the agreement system that is least susceptible to the influence of such instabilities is modifier-head agreement, particularly modifier-head agreement in oblique (non-nominative) cases. It is this type of agreement which thus is the best syntactic diagnostic of gender; including other types of agreement entails admitting (at least implicitly, and at least in Russian) nonsyntactic criteria to help determine our assignment of nouns to genders. Our definition of gender must therefore be either narrower or broader than is suggested by the most straightforward structural approach, since gender must be determined either by only some, not all, agreement patterns, or by semantic and inflexional information, and not by agreement alone.

On the basis of the information introduced above, I would conclude that both agreement and gender (to the extent that they cannot properly be identified with each other) are partly controlled both by referential and by inflexional factors. A noun of a primarily feminine-gender declension type is more likely to trigger feminine agreement than is a noun of a masculine declension type, if both are used to refer to women, and a noun that freely takes feminine agreement patterns when used to refer to women must be considered either common or feminine gender, and certainly not exclusively masculine. Roughly speaking, then, we may say that a noun of the type *sud'ja* was only unstably masculine, because of its typically feminine morphology, and now it has for many speakers fully stabilized a variable (common) gender type. On the other hand, *vrač* has highly variable agreement patterns, but is stably masculine (nonvariable) in gender. The gender-stability of *vrač* persists in the face of an obvious conflict, or inappropriateness, in its grammatical coding, and to that extent the stable masculine gender of *vrač* depends on its inflexional pattern; if it belonged to a different inflexion class, it would by now probably belong to a different gender. This situation is essentially the same as that of inanimate nouns, whose gender necessarily lacks semantic correlates and therefore depends on inflexion alone. (In the event of personification, of course, inflexion determines not only gender but also, correlatively, sex.) Finally, the basis on which the inflexion of *vrač* constrains its migration out of the masculine gender is through oblique-case modifier-head agreement; that is to say, roughly, that if feminine oblique adjective endings could appear in the same noun phrase with masculine oblique noun endings, then *vrač* would be a feminine or common gender noun, an exact counterpart of *sud'ja* or *plaksa*, which, when male-referential, appear modified by masculine oblique-case adjectives in spite of their own feminine morphology. The general, albeit asymmetrical, rule seems to be that a human male-referential noun is always masculine, but a female-referential noun is feminine only if its morphology permits. A masculine female-referential noun, however, may show feminine agreement, in certain specifiable circumstances.

Although our discussion so far hardly constitutes a full description of Russian gender, it will nonetheless provide an adequate context for our description of the animate subgender.

Any discussion of the status of animacy in the Russian gender system must take into account two striking characteristics of the animacy subgender; these characteristics can be stated as two restrictions on the range of the morphological manifestations of animacy:

(1) Animacy is a subgender only of nouns and modifiers; it is a subgender of pronouns only insofar as they are adjectival, either syntactically or inflexionally.

(2) Animacy is manifested primarily in modifier-head (oblique case) agreement, which is, as noted above, the stablest and probably most basic part of the gender-marking system.

The only exception to the general rule put forward in (2) is also exceptional according to rule (1) as well: the relative pronoun *kotoryj* does differentiate animate from inanimate antecedents through the genitive-accusative, and in this respect shows clearly its historical origin and modern inflexional status as an adjectival word. As a modifier, *kotoryj* also occurs as an indefinite interrogative, in constructions of the sort 'Kotoryj dom?', meaning 'Which house (of some small, well-defined set)?', and, in archaic usage, even the relative-pronoun construction can sometimes retain the antecedent-head noun, as in the following example from a letter of Puškin's:

(3) *Prošćajte, buďte sčastlivy, i daj Bog Vam razbogatet' s legkoj ručki xrabrogo Aleksandrova, kotoruju ručku prošu za menja pocalovat'*
'Farewell, be well, and God grant you wealth through the good offices of the brave Alexandrov, the which hand I beg you to kiss for me'. (*SjaP* 2.383)

Thus, although the relative pronoun *kotoryj* must be counted an exception to the two rules above, on the basis of its current normal usage in relative clauses, nevertheless its occurrence in indefinite constructions, its occasional occurrence in relative constructions such as (3) above, and its history and inflexional pattern all tend to make *kotoryj* less exceptional than at first appears.

To the extent that *kotoryj* is exceptional at all, it is an exception to **both** rules (1) and (2). In fact, the two restrictions listed are really interrelated, since the first restriction is actually just a corollary of the second one. If pronouns had not generalized the genitive-accusative, but instead differentiated animate from inanimate reference, the pronouns would still not display an animate subgender, any more than they now do, because pronouns would still not generally occur as heads of modifier-head constructions. (Such constructions do occur, for example with the emphatic pronoun *sam* or the quantifier *ves'* as the modifier. In such instances, the modifier regularly shows the animacy or inanimacy of its referent, or the referent of its antecedent, although it is not clear whether this marking is directly controlled by the pronoun head of the construction, instead of by the fully specified antecedent of both head and modifier. In any event, there is a well documented tendency for the modifier in such instances to be influenced by the genitive-accusative form of its head, resulting in such constructions as *vsex ix* 'all (gen.-acc.) them (gen.-acc.)' being used to refer to an inanimate object (see Blažev 1962).) Consequently, we may distinguish the fact that pronouns have generalized the genitive-accusative as the sole accusative form from the fact that the genitive-accusative does not serve to mark a subgender for pronouns; the presence of a nongeneralized genitive-accusative, such as is found in noun and adjective declension, would still not create an animate subgender for pronouns, even though it would, of course, create a semantic subclass.

We already noted in Chapters Two and Four that the pronouns seem never to have been influenced by referential animacy in their implementation of the

genitive-accusative, and that referential animacy provided a uniquely convenient differential value for the stabilization of Old Russian noun classification. We now can strengthen that observation, noting that pronouns both
historically and synchronically resist the utilization of the genitive-accusative
for purposes either of semantic classification or of syntactic gender marking,
and this resistance is to some extent at least correlated with the syntactic
nature of pronouns, to which regular participation in modifier-head relations
is nearly totally alien. Hence the difference between the utilization of the
genitive-accusative in noun or adjective declension, on the one hand, and in
pronoun declension, on the other, can be described as a function of the
syntactic differences between the two word classes, as well as of the semantic
and other differences discussed in Chapter Four. The basically correct observation that pronouns are like such semantic inanimates as *tuz* 'ace' in being
'inherently animate' regardless of their reference (see, for example, detailed
discussion in Corbett 1980a) is probably, for this reason, best re-stated in a
'semantics-free' terminology: the genitive-accusative has replaced the older
nominative-accusative everywhere in Russian declension, except where the
partial retention of the older form was syntactically functional in the gender-
coding of noun phrase elements. Hence, in Jakobsonian terms (and as implied
by Jakobson 1959/1971), it is not animacy but inanimacy that is the marked
member of the correlation, and the inflexional and syntactic behavior of the
pronouns (and of inanimates such as *tuz*) becomes completely natural.

We may thus conclude that the genitive-accusative serves to distinguish an
animate (or non-inanimate) subgender of nouns and their modifiers, where
the notion of subgender is defined as the intersection of syntactic agreement
phenomena with the Russian noun classificatory system, primarily in the
subsystem of modifier-head agreement. Animacy is lacking as a subgender of
pronouns (defining the pronouns, of course, as in Chapter One and throughout the book, on the basis of the generalized status of the genitive-accusative).
The animate subgender depends for its definition on a syntactic phenomenon
(modifier-head agreement), and the difference between the pronoun genitive-
accusative and other types of genitive-accusative is correlated with a more
general difference between the pronouns and other noun-phrase elements.
Thus, the genitive-accusative helps to articulate the syntactic properties of
pronouns as distinct from nouns or modifiers, as well as, more concretely,
helping to code noun-phrase membership of non-pronoun noun-phrase elements. The genitive-accusative thus is an element in the syntactic categoriza-
tion of Russian words, and it functions in the syntactic manifestation of gender; to this extent, then, the genitive-accusative is a syntactic phenomenon. We
may recall that the genitive-accusative also has at least a negative syntactic

function in the marking of direct objects; we concluded in Chapter Five that this syntactic aspect of the genitive-accusative arises directly out of its inherent status as an inflexional phenomenon. Similarly, the genitive-accusative functions as a syntactic gender marker precisely because of its stability in case paradigms. It is reasonable to conclude, then, that the genitive-accusative is syntactically functional precisely because of its inflexional status. The genitive-accusative, like other inflexional phenomena, articulates syntactic relations of various types: the relations of objects to verbs, of modifiers to their heads, and of one part of speech to another. A full and coherent characterization of the genitive-accusative must take into account all these aspects of the syntactic functionality of the genitive-accusative, as well as of its inflexional status. Moreover, a more nearly correct interpretation of each separate aspect of the syntactic functionality of the genitive-accusative is made possible if we keep in mind the details of the history and present status of the genitive-accusative as a whole, and not just of those aspects of the genitive-accusative that impinge on one or another subsystem of syntactic relations, such as, for example, the relations of transitive objects to the verbs that govern them.

We have seen in our own discussion that the classic view of the genitive-accusative as a marker of syntactic transitivity relations is correct only in a very special and negative sense: the genitive-accusative precisely mirrors the demise of the Old Russian system for expressing transitivity. The genitive-accusative marked (and marks) some direct objects, as well as marking other forms that are certainly not direct objects. This does not imply, however, that the genitive-accusative originated *in order* to mark direct objects. There is no good reason to treat the history of the genitive-accusative as a kind of degeneration from syntactic-communicative functionality to inflexional-grammatical nonfunctionality. On the other hand, there is rather good reason for viewing the history of the genitive-accusative as the rise of a new, primarily morphological phenomenon at the expense of an older system of object-marking. That is, the genitive-accusative was not first added to the inventory of object marking rules and then morphologized — coincidentally at the same time as the earlier object marking rules were also all being lost. Instead, the genitive-accusative itself is historically a morphologization of former genitive objects, and as such represents — inter alia — a degeneration of the Old Russian system of transitivity. There is no sense, however, in which the final shape of the Russian genitive-accusative can be called a vestige of some earlier, more functional genitive-accusative. Throughout its history, the genitive-accusative has been primarily a morphological phenomenon, although it has also had several syntactic functions. The genitive-accusative did not originate as a syntactic rule, by analogy with other syntactic rules, nor was it motivated primarily by syntactic requirements.

Bibliography

CONVENTIONS AND ABBREVIATIONS USED IN THE LISTS OF
PRIMARY SOURCE MATERIALS AND SECONDARY LITERATURE.

1. Items are listed as they are referred to in the text. In secondary literature, author and year are therefore used as headings, unless there is no author or editor. In the list of primary sources, the main listing is often given under the name of the text, although cross-references to editors' names are provided, if the editor is mentioned in the body of the book.

2. Items are listed only once. The list of secondary literature excludes titles listed among the primary sources, although some cross-listing is provided.

3. Some items are listed with several dates. Where years are separated with a slash (/), they refer to the time of the first appearance of a given work in the form cited, and a later reprint that may be more widely available. For posthumous publications, date of writing is also sometimes indicated. The annotation "1st published … " is used to provide information about publication history, where, however, the first-published edition is *not* the one cited in the body of the book; editions so annotated have not necessarily been seen by me. No attempt has been made to list prior editions of basic reference works, such as grammars.

4. The lists include only published material, except for Comrie (1976), Klein (1979), and three particularly useful doctoral dissertations (Cohen 1976, Lunt 1950, Savignac 1974). The dissertations are available through University Microfilms (Ann Arbor, Michigan). The other two papers were distributed in mimeographed form by the authors.

5. Both the list of primary sources and the list of secondary literature are selective compilations. They include all works referred to directly in the body of the book, and such works are marked with an asterisk (*). Works that are particularly useful as sources of further bibliographic material are indicated with a double asterisk (**).

ABBREVIATIONS

ASP	*Archiv für slavische Philologie*
IF	*Indogermanische Forschungen*
IORJaS	*Izvestija otdelenija russkogo jazyka i slovesnosti*
Lg	*Language*
NM	*Neuphilologische Mitteilungen* (Helsinki)
RL	*Russian Linguistics*
SEEJ	*Slavic and East European Journal*
VJa	*Voprosy jazykoznanija*
WSJ	*Wiener Slavistisches Jahrbuch*

PRIMARY SOURCE MATERIALS, INCLUDING DICTIONARIES

Akty juridičeskie ili sobranie form starinnogo deloproizvodstva.
1838   St. Petersburg: Arxeografičeskaja kommissija.
Arcixovskij, A. V.
1954   *Novgorodskie gramoty na bereste. (Iz raskopok 1954 g.)* Moscow: AN SSSR.
1963   *Novgorodskie gramoty na bereste. (Iz raskopok 1958–1961 gg.)* Moscow: Nauka.
Arcixovskij, A. V., and V. I. Borkovskij
*1958a   *Novgorodskie gramoty na bereste. (Iz raskopok 1953–1954 gg.)* Moscow: Izd-vo AN SSSR.
1958b   *Novgorodskie gramoty ne bereste. (Iz raskopok 1955 g.)* Moscow: Izd-vo AN SSSR.
*1963   *Novgorodskie gramoty na bereste. (Iz raskopok 1956–1957 gg.)* Moscow: Izd-vo AN SSSR.
Arcixovskij, A. V., and V. L. Janin
1978   *Novgorodskie gramoty na bereste. (Iz raskopok 1962–1976 gg.)* Moscow: Nauka.
Arcixovskij, A. V., and M. N. Tixomirov
1953   *Novgorodskie gramoty na bereste. (Iz raskopok 1951 g.)* Moscow: Izd-vo AN SSSR
Avanesov, R. I., ed.
*1963   *Smolenskie gramoty XIII–XIV vekov.* Moscow: AN SSSR.
Daľ, Vladimir
1880–1882/1978–1980. *Tolkovyj slovaŕ živogo velikorusskogo jazyka*, 2nd ed. St. Petersburg. Reprinted Moscow: Russkij jazyk.
Duxovnye i dogovornye gramoty velikix i udeľnyx knjazej XIII–XIV vv.
1950   Moscow: AN SSSR.
Erben, Johannes, ed.
1961   *Ostmitteldeutsche Chrestomathie.* Berlin: Akademie Verlag.
Fedotov-Čexovskij, A., ed.
1860   *Akty otnosjaščiesja do graždanskoj raspravy drevnej Rossii, I.* Kiev: Davidenko.
First Novgorod Chronicle in the Synod Manuscript, see
        Tixomirov, ed., 1964
        Nasonov, ed., 1950
        Savvaitov, ed., 1888
Grekov, V. D., ed.
*1940–1963   *Pravda Russkaja.* I. Teksty, 1940. II. Kommentarii, 1947. III. Faksimiľnoe vosproizvedenie tekstov, 1963. Moscow: AN SSSR.
Gribble, Charles E., ed.
*1973   *Medieval Slavic Texts, 1. Old and Middle Russian Texts.* Cambridge, Mass.: Slavica.
Helbig, Herbert, and Lorenz Weinrich, edd.
*1968   *Urkunden und Erzählende Quellen zur deutschen Ostsiedlung im Mittelalter, I. Mittel- und Norddeutschland. Ostseeküste.* Darmstadt: Wissenschaftliche Buchgesellschaft.
Igumen Daniil, see Seemann
Izbornik of 1076.
*1965   Edition prepared by V. S. Golyšenko, V. F. Dubrovina, V. G. Demjanov, G.

F. Nefedov, under the general editorship of S. I. Kotkov. Moscow: Nauka.

Jagić, I. V., ed.

1886 *Služebnye Minei za sentjabr', oktjabr' i nojabr' v cerkovnoslavjanskom perevode po russkim rukopisjam 1095–1097 g.* St. Petersburg: Izdanie ORJaS, AN.

Karpov, G. F., ed.

1884 *Pamjatniki diplomatičeskix snošenij Moskovskogo gosudarstva s Krymskoju i Nagajskoju ordami i s Turcieju, I: 1474–1505.* St. Petersburg: Imp. Rossijskoe Istoričeskoe Obščestvo. (Sborniki Imp. RIO, 41.)

Karskij, E., ed.

1926 *Polnoe sobranie russkix letopisej, I. 1: Lavrent'evskaja letopis'.* Leningrad: AN SSSR. Reprinted 1962 in Moscow and 1977 as volume 1 (*Die Nestorchronik*) of *Handbuch zur Nestorchronik,* Ludolf Müller, ed. Munich: Fink.

Koschmieder, Erwin

1952–1958. 'Die ältesten Novgoroder Hirmologien-Fragmente'. *Abhandlungen der Bayerischen Akademie der Wissenschaften. Philosophisch-historische Klasse.* N.F. 35 (1952), 37 (1955), 45 (1958).

*Kotošixin, see Pennington

Kurz, J., ed.

*1958– *Slovník jazyka staroslověnského. Lexicon Linguae Palaeoslovenicae.* Prague: Nakladatelství Československé Akademie Věd.

*Laurentian Manuscript of 1377

Photocopy made available through the courtesy of the Harvard Ukrainian Research Institute. See also

Karskij, ed., 1926

Povest' vremennyx let, 1872.

Lehr-Spławiński, Tadeusz, and Wiesław Witkowski, edd.

*1965 *Wybor tekstów do historii języka rosyjskiego.* Warsaw: P. Wydawnictwo naukowe.

*Life of Nifont in the Longer Redaction of 1219, see Rystenko, ed.

*Life of Savva the Enlightened, see Pomjalovskij, ed.

Meyer, Karl H.

*1935 *Altkirchenslavisch-griechisches Wörterbuch des Codex Suprasliensis.* Glückstadt: Augustin.

Napiersky, K. E., ed.

1868 *Russisch-Livländische Urkunden.* St. Petersburg: Archäographische Commission.

Nasonov, A. N., ed.

1950 *Novgorodskaja pervaja letopis' staršego i mladšego izvodov.* Moscow: AN SSSR. Reprinted in *Novgorodskaja pervaja letopis' po sinodal'nomu spisku ... with German translation and introduction by Joachim Dietze.* Munich: Sagner, 1971. (Title also in German and English.)

Nikitin, Afanasij

*1958 *Xoženie za tri morja Afanasija Nikitina 1466–1472,* 2nd ed., V. P. Adrianova-Peretc, ed. Moscow: AN SSSR.

*Novgorod Treaty with Jaroslav Jaroslavič (1270), see Šaxmatov 1885–1886.

*O Rossii v carstvovanie Alekseja Mixajloviča, see Pennington.

Ostromirovo Evangelie 1056–57 g.

*1843/1964. A. Vostokov, ed. 1st published St. Petersburg. Reprinted Wiesbaden: Harrassowitz (Monumenta Linguae Slavicae Dialecti Veteris, I).

Pomjalovskij, I., ed.

*1890   Žitie Savvy Osvjaščennogo. (Obščestvo Ljubitelej Drevnej Pis'mennosti, 96.) St. Petersburg.

Povest' vremennyx let po lavrent'evskomu spisku.

1872   St. Petersburg: Arxeografičeskaja Kommissija.

*Primary Chronicle, see Laurentian Manuscript.

*Radzivilovskaja ili kenigsbergskaja letopis'. I. Fotomexaničeskoe vosproizvedenie rukopisi.

1902   St. Petersburg: Golike and Vil'borg. (Obščestvo Ljubitelej Drevnej Pis'mennosti, 118.)

*Russkaja Pravda (1282), see Grekov, ed. 1940–1963.

Rystenko, A. V., ed.

*1928   Materialy z istorii vizantys'ko-slov'jans'koï literatury ta movy (Materialen zur Geschichte der Byzantinisch-Slavischen Literatur und Sprache.) Odessa. Pages 239–283.

Sadnik, L., and R. Aitzetmüller

1955   Handwörterbuch zu den altkirchenslavischen Texten. Heidelberg: Winter.

Savvaitov, P. I., ed.

1888   Letopis' po sinodal'nomu xaratejnomu spisku. St. Petersburg: Arxeografičeskaja Kommissija. Reprinted in Novgorodskaja pervaja letopis', Munich: Sagner, 1971. See Dietze 1971, Nasonov 1950.

Šaxmatov, A.

*1885–1886 Issledovanie o jazyke novgorodskix gramot XIII i XIV vekov. Issledovanija po russkomu jazyku, I. St. Petersburg. Pages 131–285.

Seemann, Klaus Dieter, ed.

1970   Igumen Daniil. Xoženie. Nachdruck der Ausgabe von Venevitinov 1883/85, mit einer Einleitung und bibliographischen Hinweisen. (Slavische Propyläen, 36.) Munich: Fink.

Sever'janov, S., ed.

*1904/1956 Codex Suprasliensis (I-II). Graz: Akademische Druck- u. Verlagsanstalt. (Ed. monumentorum slavicorum veteris dialecti.) 1st published 1904 in St. Petersburg.

*1922/1954 Sinajskij Psaltyr'. Graz: Akademische Druck- u. Verlagsanstalt. (Ed. monumentorum slavicorum veteris dialecti.) 1st published 1922 in Petrograd.

Sinajskij Paterik.

*1967   Edition prepared by V. S. Golyšenko and V. F. Dubrovina, under the general editorship of S. I. Kotkov. Moscow: Nauka.

*Sinai Psalter, see Sever'janov 1922/1954.

*Slovar' jazyka Puškina v 4x tomax

1956–1961 Moscow: Gos. izd-vo inostrannyx i nacional'nyx slovarej. (AN SSSR, In-t jazykoznanija.)

Slovar' sovremennogo russkogo literaturnogo jazyka v 17 tomax.

1949–1965 Moscow: AN SSSR.

*Slovník jazyka staroslověnského, see Kurz, ed., 1958–

*Smolensk trade treaties, see Avanesov, ed., 1963.

Sreznevskij, I. I.
*1893–1903 *Materialy dlja slovarja drevne-russkogo jazyka,* I (1893), II (1895), III (1903). St. Petersburg: AN.
*Suprasliensis, see Severʹjanov 1904/1956
*Suzdal Chronicle, see Laurentian Manuscript of 1377
*Synod Manuscript, see First Novgorod Chronicle
Tixomirov, N., ed.
1964 *Novgorodskaja xaratejnaja letopis'.* Moscow: Nauka.
Tupikov, N. M.
1903 *Slovar' drevne-russkix ličnyx sobstvennyx imen. (Zapiski russkogo otdelenija imperatorskogo arxeografičeskogo obščestva.)* St. Petersburg: Skoroxodov.
Uspenskij Sbornik XII–XIII vv.
*1971 Edition prepared by O. A. Knjazevskaja, V. G. Demʹjanov, M. V. Ljapon, under the general editorship of S. I. Kotkov. Moscow: Nauka.
Valk, S. N.
*1949 *Gramoty Velikogo Novgoroda i Pskova.* Moscow: AN SSSR. Reprinted Brücken-Verlag (Düsseldorf) and Europe-Printing (Vaduz), 1970.
van den Baar, A. H., ed.
1968 *A Russian Church Slavonic Kanonnik (1331–1332).* The Hague: Mouton.
Vondrák, V., ed.
1925 *Církevněslovanská Chrestomatie.* Brno: Píša.
*Vostokov, A., ed., see Ostromirovo Evangelie
Vygoleksinskij Sbornik
*1977 Edition prepared by V. F. Dubrovina, R. V. Baxturina, and V. S. Golyšenko, under the general editorship of S. I. Kotkov. Moscow: Nauka.
Xoženie za tri morja, see Nikitin

SECONDARY LITERATURE

Aleškovskij, M. X.
1971 *Povest' vremennyx let. Sud'ba literaturnogo proizvedenija v drevnej Rusi.* Moscow: Nauka.
Andersen, Henning
1973 'Abductive and Deductive Change'. *Lg.* 49.765–793.
*1980 'Morphological Change: towards a Typology'. *Recent Developments in Historical Morphology,* Jacek Fisiak, ed. The Hague: Mouton. Pages 1–50.
Anderson, S., and P. Kiparsky, edd.
1973 *A Festschrift for Morris Halle.* New York: Holt.
Avanesov, R. I., and V. G. Orlova
*1965 *Russkaja dialektologija.* Moscow: Nauka.
Bělič, Jaromír
1977 'Bez něj je to těžké'. *Naše řeč* 2.57–67.
Benninghoven, F.
1961 'Rigas Entstehung und der frühansische Kaufmann'. *Nord- und Osteuropäische Geschichtsstudien,* 3. Hamburg.
Berneker, E.

1900   *Die Wortfolge in den slavischen Sprachen.* Berlin: Behr.
*1904   'Der genetiv-accusativ bei belebten wesen im Slavischen'. *Zeitschrift für vergleichende Sprachforschung auf dem Gebiete der Indogermanischen Sprachen, begründet von A. Kuhn.* 37 (n. F. 17).364–386.
Black, Max
1968   *The Labyrinth of Language.* New York: American Library (Mentor).
Blažev, B.
*1962   'Slučai transponirovanija form oduševlennosti u nekotoryx opredeliteľnyx mestoimenij i čisliteľnyx v russkom jazyke'. *Russkij jazyk v nacionaľnoj škole* 3.29–34.
Bloomfield, Leonard
1933   *Language.* New York: Holt.
Borkovskij, V. I.
*1949   *Sintaksis drevnerusskix gramot (prostoe predloženie).* Ľvov: Ľvovskij gos. un-t.
Bondarko, A. V.
1976   'K interpretacii oduševlennosti-neoduševlennosti, razrjadov pola i kategorii roda (na materiale russkogo jazyka)'. *Slavjanskoe i balkanskoe jazykoznanie.* Moscow: Nauka. Pages 25–39.
The Cambridge Medieval History, volume VII.
1932   Chapters VIII ('The Hansa', A. Weiner), 216–247; IX ('The Teutonic Order', A. Boswell), 248–269; XXI ('Russia', D. S. Mirsky), 599–631. Cambridge: University Press.
Chvany, Catherine V., and Richard Brecht, edd.
1980   *Morphosyntax in Slavic.* Columbus, Ohio: Slavica.
Coats, Herbert S.
1978   'A Study of Inflectional Change: The Genitive-Accusative in East Slavic'. *American Contributions to the 8th International Congress of Slavists, I (Linguistics and Poetics),* Henrik Birnbaum, ed. Columbus, Ohio: Slavica. Pages 234–255.
Cocron, Friedrich
*1962   *La langue russe dans la seconde moitié du XVIIe siècle (morphologie).* Paris: In-t d'études slaves de l'université de Paris.
Cohen, William David
*1976   *The Laurentian Version of the Suzdaľ Chronicle: A Morphological Study.* Unpublished Ph.D. dissertation, University of Michigan (Ann Arbor), Department of Slavic Languages and Literatures.
Comrie, Bernard S.
*1976   'Marked Syntactic Relations: Diachronic Syntax and Morphology'. Ms.
*1978a 'Genitive-Accusatives in Slavic: the Rules and Their Motivation'. *International Review of Slavic Linguistics* 3.27–42.
1978b   'Sex, Gender, and the Status of Women'. Comrie and Stone, 159–171.
Comrie, Bernard S., and Gerald Stone
1978   *The Russian Language since the Revolution.* Oxford: Clarendon.
Corbett, Greville G.
*1979   'The Agreement Hierarchy'. *Journal of Linguistics* 15.203–224.
*1980a 'Animacy in Russian and Other Slavonic Languages: Where Syntax and

Semantics Fail to Match'. Chvany and Brecht, edd., 43–61.
1980b 'Naturalness and Markedness of Morphological Rules: the Problem of Animacy in Russian'. *Wiener Slawistischer Almanach* 6.251–260.
**1982 'Gender in Russian: an Account of Gender Specification and Its Relationship to Declension'. *RL* 2.197–232.

Crockett, Dina B.
1976 *Agreement in Contemporary Standard Russian.* Columbus, Ohio: Slavica.

Delbrück, B.
*1893 *Vergleichende Syntax der indogermanischen Sprachen*, I. Strassburg: Trübner.

Demidova, G. I.
1958 'Iz istorii form imeniteľnogo padeža množestvennogo čisla imen suščestviteľnyx v russkom jazyke XII–XVII vv.' *Učenye zapiski Leningradskogo gos. ped. in-ta im. A. I. Gercena. Kafedra russkogo jazyka.* 144.145–166.

Diels, Paul
1932–1934 *Altkirchenslavische Grammatik.* Heidelberg: Winter.

Dietze, Joachim
1971 'Introduction' to *The First Novgorod Chronicle in Its Oldest Version (Synodal Transcript) 1016–1333/1352.* Munich: Sagner. Pages 7–47.
*1973 'Die Entwicklung der altrussischen Kategorie der Beseeltheit im 13. und 14. Jahrhundert'. *Zeitschrift für Slawistik* 18.261–272.
*1975 *Die Sprache der Ersten Novgoroder Chronik. Die von der Synodalhandschrift graphisch reflektierte phonetische und phonologische Situation.* Poznań: Uniwersytet im. A. Mickiewicz. (Seria filologia rosyjska, 6.)

Dostál, Antonín
*1954 *Studie o vidovém systému v staroslověnštině.* Prague: Státní ped. naklad.

Durnovo, Nikolaj (Nicolas)
*1924 'La catégorie du genre en russe moderne'. *Revue des Études slaves* 4 (1–2).208–221.
*1924/1962 *Očerk istorii russkogo jazyka.* 1st published Moscow and Leningrad. Reprinted at The Hague: Mouton. (Slavistic Printings and Reprintings, 22.)
*1927 *Vvedenie v istoriju russkogo jazyka.* Brno. Reprinted at The Hague: Mouton
** (Slavistic Printings and Reprintings, 122), 1970. 2nd ed., with additions and commentary by L. L. Kasatkin and T. S. Sumnikova, published in Moscow: Nauka, 1969.

Elenskij, J.
**1977 'O kategorii oduševlennosti v russkom jazyke'. *Bolgarskaja rusistika* 6.41–54.

Fenne, Tönnies
1607/1970 *Low German Manual of Spoken Russian*, 2. L. L. Hammerich and R. O. Jakobson, edd. Copenhagen: Commissioner. (Royal Danish Academy of Sciences and Letters.)

Filin, F. P.
*1972 *Proisxoždenie russkogo, ukrainskogo i belorusskogo jazykov. Istoriko-dialektologičeskij očerk.* Leningrad: Nauka.

Fodor, I.
1952 'The Origin of Grammatical Gender'. *Lingua* 8.1–41, 186–214.

Frink, Orrin
1962 'Genitive-Accusative in the Laurentian Primary Chronicle'. *SEEJ* 6.133–137.

Gabrielsson, Artur
1971   'Zur Geschichte der mittelniederdeutschen Schriftsprache auf Gotland, 1'.
        Niederdeutsches Jahrbuch 94.41–82.
Gadolina, Margarita A.
1963   *Istorija form ličnyx i vozvratnogo mestoimenij v slavjanskix jazykax.* Moscow:
        Izd-vo AN SSSR. (In-t Slavjanovedenija.)
Gancov, V. M.
1927   'Osobennosti jazyka Radzivilovskogo (Kenigsbergskogo) spiska letopisi'.
        IORJaS 32.177–242.
Gladkij, A. V.
*1969   'K opredeleniju ponjatij padeža i roda suščestviteľnogo'. *VJa* 2.110–123.
*1973   'Popytka formaľnogo opredelenija ponjatij padeža i roda suščestviteľnogo'.
        Problemy grammatičeskogo modelirovanija. Moscow: Nauka. Pages 24–53.
Goetz, Leopold Karl
*1916   *Deutsch-Russische Handelsverträge des Mittelalters.* Hamburg: L. Friederich-
        sen.
Golyšenko, V. S.
*1977   'Vvedenie'. *Vygoleksinskijj Sbornik,* 7–66.
Goodwin, W. S.
*1930   *Greek Grammar* (revised by C. B. Gulick). Boston: Ginn.
Grappin, Henri
1956   *Histoire de la flexion du nom en polonais.* Wrocław: Ossolineum.
Greenberg, Joseph
**1957 'Structure and Function in Language'. *Essays in Linguistics.* Chicago: U.
        Chicago. Pages 75–85.
*1978   'How Does a Language Acquire Gender Markers?' *Universals of Human
        Language, 3: Word Structure,* Joseph Greenberg, ed. Stanford, California:
        Stanford U. Pages 47–82.
Grünenthal, O.
*1910–1911 'Die Übersetzungstechnik der altkirchenslavischen Evangelienüberset-
        zung'. *ASP* 31(1910).321–66, 507–28; 32(1911).1–48.
Güldenstubbe, O. v.
1923   'Gebrauch der Kasus im Altrussischen'. *ASP* 38.150–181.
Hall, G. L., and J. St.-Clair-Sobell
1954   'Animate Gender in Slavonic and Romance Languages'. *Lingua* 4.194–206.
Hammerich, L. L., and R. O. Jakobson
1970   'Preface'. *Tönnies Fenne's Low German Manual of Spoken Russian.* (see Fenne,
        Tönnies.) Pages VII–XXVIII.
Havránek, Bohuslav
1928–1937 *Genera verbi v slovanských jazycích,* I (1928) and II (1937). Prague:
        Česká spol. nauk.
Hjelmslev, Louis
*1956/1959 'Animé et inanimé, personnel et non-personnel'. *Essais linguistiques.
        Travaux du Cercle Linguistique de Copenhague* 12(1959).211–249. 1st pub-
        lished in *Travaux de l'Institut de linguistique,* I (Paris, 1956), 155–199.
Hockett, Charles
1961   'Grammar for the Hearer'. *Structure of Language and Its Mathematical*

Aspects (Proceedings of Symposia in Applied Mathematics, 12.), Roman Jakobson, ed. Providence, R.I.: American Mathematical Society. Pages 220–236.

Hopper, Paul, and Sandra A. Thompson
*1980 'Transitivity in Grammar and Discourse'. *Lg* 56.251–299.

Hüttl-Folter, see Hüttl-Worth

Hüttl-Worth, Gerta
*1973 (Xjutl'-Vort, G.) 'Spornye problemy izučenija literaturnogo jazyka v drevnerusskij period'. *WSJ* 18.29–47.
*1980 (Hüttl-Folter, Gerta) 'Zur Sprache der Nestorchronik: Russisch-kirchenslavisch-altrussische lexikalische Wechselbeziehungen'. *Zeitschrift für Slavische Philologie* 41.1.34–57.

Ickovič, V. A.
*1980 'Suščestviteľnye oduševlennye i neoduševlennye v sovremennom russkom jazyke (norma i tendencija)'. *VJa* 4.84–96.

Isačenko, Alexander
1970 'East Slavic Morphophonemics and the Treatment of the Jers in Russian: a Revision of Havlík's Law'. *International Journal of Slavic Linguistics and Poetics,* 13.73–124.
1980 (Issatschenko, Alexander) *Geschichte der russischen Sprache, I. Von den Anfängen bis zum Ende des 17. Jahrhunderts.* Heidelberg: Winter.

Issatschenko, see Isačenko

Istrina, E. S.
*1923 'Sintaksičeskie javlenija Sinodaľnogo spiska I Novgorodskoj letopisi'. *IORJaS* 24(1919). 2.1–172; 26(1921). 207–239.

Jakobson, Roman Osipovič
1936/1971 'Beitrag zur allgemeinen Kasuslehre: Gesamtbedeutungen der russischen Kasus'. *Selected Writings,* II (q.v.)23–71. 1st published in *Travaux du Cercle Linguistique de Prague*, 6 (1936).
1958/1971 'Morfologičeskie nabljudenija nad slavjanskim skloneniem.' *Selected Writings*, II (q.v.).154–183. 1st published in the *American Contributions to the 4th International Congress of Slavists, held in Moscow, September 1958.* The Hague: Mouton. Pages 127–156.
*1959/1971 'On the Rumanian Neuter'. *Selected Writings*, II (q.v.).187–189. Written 1959 for *Mélanges Linguistiques offerts à Emil Petrovici = Cercetări de Lingvistică*, 3.
*1960/1971 'The Gender Pattern of Russian'. *Selected Writings*, II (q.v.).184–186. 1st published in *Studii şi Cercetări Lingvistice (Omagiu lui Al. Graur),* 11, 1960.
*1971 *Selected Writings, II. Word and Language.* The Hague: Mouton.

Joos, Martin
1950 'Description of Language Design'. *Journal of the Acoustical Society of America,* 22.701–708.

Karcevskij, S.
1932/1964 'De la structure du substantif russe'. *Charisteria Guilelmo Mathesio ... oblata.* Prague: Pražský Linguistický Kroužek. Pages 65–73. Reprinted in *A Prague School Reader in Linguistics*, J. Vachek, ed., Bloomington, Indiana: Indiana Univ. Pages 335–346.

Karpinskaja, O. G.
*1964 'Tipologija roda v slavjanskix jazykax'. *VJa*, 6.61–76.
*1966 'Metody tipologičeskogo opisanija slavjanskix rodovyx sistem'. *Lingvističe-
** skie issledovanija po obščej i slavjanskoj tipologii.* Moscow: Nauka. Pages 75–115.

1973   (Revzina, O. G.) 'Obščaja teorija grammatičeskix kategorij'. *Strukturno-tipologičeskie issledovanija v oblasti grammatiki slavjanskix jazykov.* Moscow: Nauka. Pages 5–38.

Karskij, E. F.

1893/1962 'Glavnejšie tečenija v russkom literaturnom jazyke'. *Trudy po belorusskomu i drugim slavjanskim jazykam.* Moscow: AN SSSR. Pages 130–138. 1st published 1893 in Warsaw.

1929/1962 'Nabljudenija v oblasti sintaksisa Lavreńevskogo spiska letopisi'. *IOR-JaS* 2.1.1–71. Reprinted in E. F. Karskij, *Trudy po belorusskomu i drugim slavjanskim jazykam.* Moscow: AN SSSR. Pages 58–112.

1962   'Russkaja Pravda po drevnejšemu spisku'. *Trudy po belorusskomu i drugim slavjanskim jazykam.* Moscow: AN SSSR. Pages 113–129. Abridged from work 1st published 1930.

Kedajtene, E. I.

1955   'Iz nabljudenij nad kategoriej lica v pamjatnikax russkogo jazyka staršej pory'. *VJa* 1.124–128.

*1961   'K voprosu o razvitii form roditeľnogo-viniteľnogo padeža (na materiale vostočnoslavjanskix jazykov)'. *Issledovanija po leksikologii i grammatike russkogo jazyka.* Moscow: AN SSSR. Pages 185–193.

Kiparsky, Valentin

*1939   (Review of) 'G. Schmidt. *Das Eindringen der hochdeutschen Schriftsprache in der Rigaschen Ratskanzlei'. NM* 40.1.83–87.

*1960   'Wer hat den Handelsvertrag zwischen Smolensk und Riga vom J. 1229 aufgesetzt?' *NM* 61.2.244–248.

**1963–1975 *Russische historische Grammatik,* I (1963), II (1967), III (1975). Heidelberg: Winter.

Klein, Flora

1979   'Neuterality, or the Semantics of Gender in a Dialect of Castilla'. Paper presented at the Linguistic Symposium on Romance Languages, Georgetown University.

Klenin, Emily

*1980a 'Conditions on Object Marking'. *Papers from the 4th International Conference on Historical Linguistics,* Elizabeth C. Traugott et al., edd. Amsterdam: Benjamins. Pages 253–258.

*1980b 'Individuation: an Historical Case Study'. Chvany and Brecht, edd., 62–78.

*1980c 'On the Genitive-Accusative of Anaphoric Pronouns in the Laurentian Manuscript of 1377'. *SEEJ* 24.52–62.

*1983   'The Genitive-Accusative as a Slavonicism in the Laurentian Manuscript: the Problem of Text Segmentation'. *American Contributions to the 9th International Congress of Slavists, Kiev, 1983. I. Linguistics.* M. S. Flier, ed. (In press.)

Knjazevskaja, O. A.

*1971   'Vremja i mesto napisanija rukopisi'. *Uspenskij Sbornik.* Pages 24–26.

Kočin, G. E.

*1939   'O dogovorax Novgoroda s knjazjami'. *Učenye zapiski Leningradskogo gos. ped. in-ta im. A. I. Gercena,* 19.199–210.

Kolessa, A.

1896   'Dialektologische Merkmale des südrussischen Denkmals "Žitije sv. Savy"'. *ASP* 18.203–228, 473–523.

Kopeliovič, A. B.
1977 'K voprosu o kodifikacii imen suščestviteľnyx obščego roda'. *Grammatika i norma*, V. A. Ickovič, G. I. Mis̆kevič, and L. I. Skvorcov, edd. Moscow: Nauka. Pages 178–192.

Korlén, Gustav
1945 *Die mnd. Texte des XIII Jahrhunderts. (Lunder Germanistische Forschungen, 18.)*

Kucała, Marian
**1978 *Rodzaj gramatyczny w historii polszczyzny.* Wrocław: PAN. (Prace Instytutu języka polskiego, 23.)

Kulikov, V. B.
1959 'Imennoe sklonenie v pamjatnikax pis̆mennosti severo-vostočnoj Rusi konca XIV – načalo XVI v.' *Trudy Uzbekskogo gos. un-ta. im. A. Navoi* (Samarkand), nov. ser. 95.77–119.

Kuno, Susumu
*1975 'Subject, Theme, and the Speaker's Empathy — a Reexamination of Relativization Phenomena'. *Subject and Topic*, Charles N. Li, ed. New York: Academic Press (Harcourt Brace Jovanovich). Pages 417–444.

Kuryłowicz, Jerzy
1934/1960 'W sprawie genezy rodzaju gramatycznego'. *Esquisses linguistiques (Prace językoznawcze, 19).* Wrocław: PAN. Pages 151–154. 1st published in *Sprawozdania Polskeij Akademii Umiejętności,* 10(1934).5–8.

1947/1960 'Męski acc.-gen. i nom.-acc. w języku polskim'. *Esquisses linguistiques (Prace językoznawcze, 19).* Wrocław: PAN. Pages 155–159. 1st published in *Sprawozdania Polskiej Akademii Umiejętności,* 1947.12–16.

*1962 'Personal and Animate Genders in Slavic'. *Lingua* 11.249–255.

Kuźmina, I. B., and E. V. Nemčenko
*1964 'K voprosu o konstrukcijax s formoj imeniteľnogo padeža imeni pri perexodnyx glagolax i pri predikativnyx narečijax v russkix govorax'. *Voprosy dialektologii vostočnoslavjanskix jazykov,* R. I. Avanesov, ed. Moscow: Nauka. Pages 151–175.

Kuznecov, P. S.
*1965 'Morfologija'. *Istoričeskaja grammatika russkogo jazyka* (2nd ed.), by Viktor I. Borkovskij and P. S. Kuznecov. Moscow: Nauka. Pages 171–337.

Lasch, Agathe
*1914 *Mittelniederdeutsche Grammatik.* (Sammlung kurzer Grammatiken germanischer Dialekte, 9.) Halle a. S.: Niemeyer.

Lavrov, B. V.
1941 *Uslovnye i ustupiteľnye predloženija v drevnerusskom jazyke.* Moscow: Izd-vo AN SSSR.

Leskien, A.
1969 *Handbuch der altbulgarischen (altkirchenslavischen Sprache),* 9th ed. Heidelberg: Winter.

Lixačev, D. S.
1947/1966 *Russkie letopisi i ix kuľturno-istoričeskoe značenie.* Moscow: Izd-vo AN SSSR. Reprinted at The Hague: Europe Printing.

Ljapunov, B. M.
1916 'Professor A. V. Rystenko i napečatannye im teksty žitija Nifonta'. *Izvestija*

Odesskogo bibligrafičeskogo obščestva pri imperatorskom rossijskom unte., 5.3–6.85–103.

Lunt, Horace G.
1950   *The Orthography of 11th-Century Russian Manuscripts.* Ph.D. dissertation, Columbia University, Department of Slavic Languages and Literatures.
*1974   *Old Church Slavonic Grammar,* 6th ed. The Hague: Mouton.
1975   'On the Languages of Old Rus': Some Questions and Suggestions'. *RL* 2.269–281.

Marcus, Solomon
1962   'Le genre grammatical et son modèle logique'. *Cahiers de linguistique théorique et appliquée* 1.103–122.
1963   'A Synchronic Analysis of the Grammatical Gender'. *Revue (Roumaine) de linguistique* 8.1.99–111.

Mareš, František Václav
*1967   'The Historic Development of the Slavic Noun Declension, I. The System of Categories'. *Slavia* 36.485–506.

Meillet, Antoine
*1897   *Du genre animé en vieux-slave et de ses origines indo-européennes. Thèse présentée à la faculté des lettres de Paris.* Paris: Bouillon. = *Recherches sur l'emploi du génitif-accusatif en vieux-slave.* (Bibliothèque de l'École des Hautes études, 115.)
*1934/1965 *Le slave commun* (2nd ed., revised and enlarged with the aid of A. Vaillant). Paris: Champion. 1st edition 1924.

Mel'čuk, Igor A.
1980   'Animacy in Russian Cardinal Numerals and Adjectives as an Inflectional Category'. *Lg* 56.797–811.

Miklosich, Franz
*1883   *Vergleichende Grammatik der slavischen Sprachen, IV. Syntax.* Vienna: Braumüller.

Mjulenbax, Karl
1899   'Ob upotreblenii roditel'nogo padeža vmesto vinitel'nogo v slavjanskix jazykax'. *IORJaS* 4.1192–1217.

Moravcsik, Edith A.
1978   'Agreement'. *Universals of Human Language, 4: Syntax,* Joseph H. Greenberg, ed. Stanford, California: Stanford University. Pages 331–374.

Mučnik, I. P.
1971   *Grammatičeskie kategorii glagola i imeni v sovremennom russkom literaturnom jazyke.* Moscow: Nauka.

Müller, Klaus
1965   *Die Beseeltheit in der Grammatik der russischen Sprache der Gegenwart und ihre historische Entwicklung.* = *Sitzungsberichte der DAK zu Berlin, Klasse für Sprachen, Literatur und Kunst,* 1965, No. 2.

Nekrasov, N. P.
1897   *Zametki o jazyke "Povesti vremennyx let" po Lavrent'evskomu spisku letopisi.* St. Petersburg: Imperatorskaja AN.
*1905   O zamenitel'nyx padežax: roditel'nom i vinitel'nom v sovremennom russkom jazyke. *IORJaS* 10.1.31–65.

1909   'Po povodu dvux statej A. I. Tomsona o rod.-vin. padeže'. *IORJaS*
       14.3.35–74.

Nissen, Carl A.
*1884   *Forssøg til en middelnedertysk syntax.* Copenhagen: Kommission, Priors.

Oberpfalcer, F.
1932   'Mužský rod o ženách v češtině'. *Charisteria Guilelmo Mathesio ... oblata.*
       Prague: Pražský Linguistický Kroužek. Pages 85–91.

Obnorskij, S. P.
1934/1960   '"Russkaja Pravda", kak pamjatnik russkogo literaturnogo jazyka'.
       Izbrannye raboty po russkomu jazyku. Moscow: Gos. uč-ped. izd-vo. Pages
       120–144. 1st published in *Izvestija* AN SSSR. OON, No. 10. 749–776.

Paleografičeskij i lingvističeskij analiz Novgorodskix berestjanyx gramot.
1955   Moscow: Izd-vo AN SSSR. (In-t jazykoznanija.)

Panov, M. V.
*1968   *Russkij jazyk i sovetskoe obščestvo, III. Morfologija i sintaksis so-
       vremennogo russkogo literaturnogo jazyka.* Moscow: Nauka.

Pennington, Anne E., ed.
*1980   *Grigorij Kotošixin. O Rossii v carstvovanie Alekseja Mixajloviča. Russia in the
       Reign of Aleksej Mixajlovič.* Oxford: Clarendon.

Perlmutter, David, and J. Orešnik
1973   'Language-Particular Rules and Explanation in Syntax'. S. Anderson and P.
       Kiparsky, edd. Pages 419–459.

Peškovskij, A. M.
1928/1956   *Russkij sintaksis v naučnom osveščenii,* 7th ed. Moscow: Gos. uč-ped.
       izd-vo. (1956 reprint of 4th ed., which is a corrected reprint of the 3rd ed. of
       1928, completed 1927.)

Priselkov, M. D.
*1940/1966   *Istorija russkogo letopisanija XI–XV vv.* Leningrad: Leningradskij gos.
       un-t. Reprinted at The Hague: Europe Printing. (Russian Reprint Series, 17.)

Proxorov, G. M.
*1972   'Kodikologičeskij analiz Lavrenťevskoj letopisi'. *Vspomogateľnye istoričeskie
       discipliny,* IV. Leningrad: Nauka. Pages 77–104.

Rastorguev, P. A.
1960   *Govory na territorii Smolenščiny.* Moscow: AN SSSR.

Revzin, I. I.
1967   *Metod modelirovanija i tipologija slavjanskix jazykov.* Moscow: Nauka.
*1977   *Sovremennaja strukturnaja lingvistika: problemy i metody.* Moscow: Nauka.

Revzina, see Karpinskaja

Rosetti, A.
1964   'Sur la catégorie du neutre'. *Proceedings of the 9th International Congress of
       Linguists.*The Hague: Mouton. Pages 778–783.

Rösler, Karl
1952   'Beobachtungen und Gedanken über das analytische Futurum in Slavischen'.
       2.103–149.

Rothstein, Robert
1973   'Sex, Gender, and the October Revolution'. S. Anderson and P.
       Kiparsky, edd.. Pages 460–466.

1976 'Uwagi o rodzaju gramatycznym i cechach semantycznych wyrazów'. *Język Polski* 56.241–253.

*1980 'Gender and Reference in Polish and Russian'. Chvany and Brecht, edd.
** Pages 79–97.

Russkaja Grammatika, I–II.

1980 Moscow: Nauka.

Savignac, David T.

*1974 *A History of the Pronominal Declension in the Novgorod Dialect of Old Russian*
** *from the 11th to the 16th Centuries.* Ph.D. dissertation, Stanford University, Department of Slavic Languages and Literatures.

Šaxmatov, A. A.

*1910–1911/1957/1976 *Istoričeskaja morfologija russkogo jazyka.* Moscow: Gos. uč-ped. izd-vo, 1957. Written 1910–1911 as an academic lecture series. Reprinted Leipzig: Zentralantiquariat, 1976.

*1925 *Očerk sovremennogo russkogo literaturnogo jazyka.* Leningrad: Gos. izd-vo. (Lengiz.) Reprinted at The Hague: Mouton, 1969 (Slavistic Printings and Reprintings, 125).

*1938/1968 *Obozrenie russkix letopisnyx svodov XIV–XVI vv.* Moscow: AN SSSR. Reprinted Brücken-Verlag and Europe Printing at Düsseldorf and The Hague.

1941 *Sintaksis russkogo jazyka*, 2nd ed., edited and with commentaries by E. S. Istrina. Leningrad: Gos. uč-ped. izd-vo. Narkomprosa RSFSR.

Ščerba, L. V.

1928/1974 'O častjax reči v russkom jazyke'. *Jazykovaja sistema i rečevaja dejatel'-nost'.* Leningrad: Nauka. Pages 77–100. 1st published in *Russkaja reč,* nov. ser. 2 (1928).5–27. (Leningrad)

Schenker, Alexander

1955 'Gender categories in Polish'. *Lg* 31.402–408.

Seliščev, A. M.

*1941/1957/1968 'O jazyke "Russkoj Pravdy" v svjazi s voprosom o drevnejšem tipe russkogo literaturnogo jazyka'. *Izbrannye trudy.* Moscow: Prosveščenie. Pages 129–140. 1st published posthumously in *VJa* 1957, No. 4.

Shevelov, George

*1968 'On the Lexical Make-Up of the Galician-Volhynian Chronicle. An Experiment in the Comprehensive Study of Vocabulary followed by a Few Remarks on the Literary Language of Old Rus''. *Studies in Slavic Linguistics and Poetics in Honor of Boris O. Unbegaun,* R. Magidoff et al., edd. New York: New York University. Pages 195–207.

Silverstein, Michael

1977 'Hierarchy of Features and Ergativity'. *Grammatical Categories in Australian Languages.* Canberra: Australian Institute for Aboriginal Studies. Pages 112–171.

Skoblikova, E. S.

1971 *Soglasovanie i upravlenie v russkom jazyke.* Moscow: Prosveščenie.

Šmeleva, I. N.

1974 'Priloženie'. *Trudnosti slovoupotreblenija i varianty norm russkogo literaturnogo jazyka: slovar'-spravočnik,* K. S. Gorbačevič, ed. Leningrad: Nauka. Pages 511–518.

Sobolevskij, A. I.
*1907/1962 *Lekcii po istorii russkogo jazyka,* 4th ed. (Moscow), reprinted at The Hague: Mouton.

Sommer, Ferdinand
*1916 'Zur Syntax des slavischen Genitiv-Akkusativ bei belebten Wesen'. *IF* 36.302–319.

Sørensen, H. Chr.
*1959 'Zur Verallgemeinerung der Endungen -am, -ami, -ach im Russischen'. *Scando-Slavica* 4.87–120.

Stang, Chr. S.
1939 *Die altrussische Urkundensprache der Stadt Polozk.* (= Skrifter utgitt av det Norske Videnskaps-akademi i Oslo, Hist.-filos. Klasse, 1938, 2, 9).

Stankiewicz, Edward
*1968a *Declension and Gradation of Russian Substantives.* The Hague: Mouton.
1968b 'The Grammatical Genders of the Slavic Languages'. *International Journal of Slavic Linguistics and Poetics* 11.27–41.

Stepanov, Ju. S.
**1975 *Metody i principy sovremennoj lingvistiki.* Moscow: Nauka.

Stieber, Zdisław
1973 *Zarys gramatyki porównawczej języków słowiańskich, cz. 2,2. Fleksja verbalna.* Warsaw: P. Wydawnictwo naukowe.

Stieda, Wilhelm
*1885 'Zur Sprachkenntniss der Hanseaten'. *Hansische Geschichtsblätter* XIII (Jg. 1884).157–161. Leipzig.

Stone, Gerald
*1978 'Morphology'. Comrie and Stone, Pages 73–101.

Sumnikova, T. A.
*1963 'Vvedenie' and commentaries to all texts in Avanesov, ed., 1963.
**

Švedova, N. Ju., ed.
1970 *Grammatika sovremennogo russkogo literaturnogo jazyka.* Moscow: Nauka.

Thomason, Sarah Gray
1976 'Analogic Change as Grammar Complication'. *Current Progress in Historical Linguistics,* W. Christie, ed. Amsterdam: North Holland. Pages 401–409.

Thomson, A. I.
*1908 (Tomson, A. I.) 'Roditeľnyj-viniteľnyj padež pri nazvanijax živyx suščestv v
** slavjanskix jazykax'. *IORJaS* 13.2.232–264.
*1909 (Tomson, A. I.) 'K voprosu o vozniknovenii rod.-vin. p. v slavjanskix jazykax'. *IORJaS,* ser. 2, 14.1.59–83.
1909–1912 'Beiträge zur Kasuslehre'. *IF* 24(1909).293–307; 28(1911).104–120; 29(1911).249–259; 30(1912).65–79.
*1913 (Tomson, A. I.) 'Proisxoždenie form im. i vin. p. i grammatičeskogo roda v indoevropejskom prajazyke'. *IORJaS,* ser. 2, 18.4.148–172.

Timberlake, Alan
*1974 *The Nominative Object in Slavic, Baltic, and West Finnic.* Munich: Sagner. (Slavistische Beiträge, 82.)
*1975 'Hierarchies in the Genitive of Negation'. *SEEJ* 19.123–139.

Timčenko, E. K.
1913   'Funkcii genetiva v južnorusskoj jazykovoj oblasti'. *Russkij filologičeskij vestnik* 69.207–223, 261–340; 70.1–70, 185–220, 1–74.
Tixomirov, M. N.
1956   *Drevnerusskie goroda* (2nd ed.) Moscow: Gos. izd-vo polit. lit.
Tomson, see Thomson
Tymčenko, see Timčenko
Unbegaun, Boris O.
*1935 *La langue russe au XVIe siècle (1500–1550). I. La flexion des noms.* Thèse pour le doctorat ès lettres presentée à la faculté des lettres de l'université de Paris. Paris: Champion.
Uspenskij, Boris A.
*1976 'K voprosu o semantičeskix vzaimootnošenijax sistemno protivopostavlennyx cerkovnoslavjanskix i russkix form v istorii russkogo jazyka'. *WSJ* 22.92–100.
Vaillant, André
*1964 *Manuel du vieux slave, I. Grammaire,* 2nd ed. Paris: In-t d'Études slaves.
van Schooneveld, Cornelius H.
*1977 'The Place of Gender in the Semantic Structure of the Russian Language'. *Scando-Slavica* 23.129–138.
van Wijk, N.
*1931 *Geschichte der altkirchenslavischen Sprache, I. Laut- und Formenlehre.* Berlin: de Gruyter.
Večerka, R.
*1963 'Sintaksis bespredložnogo roditeľnogo padeža v staroslavjanskom jazyke'. *Issledovanija po sintaksisu staroslavjanskogo jazyka,* J. Kurz, ed. Prague: Czechoslovak Academy of Sciences. Pages 183–223.
Vinogradov, V. V.
1947/1972 *Russkij jazyk.* Moscow: Vysšaja škola.
*1968 'Orfografija i jazyk Žitija Savvy Osvjaščennogo po rukopisi XIII v.'. *Pamjatniki drevnerusskoj pis'mennosti. Jazyk i tekstologija,* V. V. Vinogradov, ed., Moscow: Nauka. Pages 137–198.
Vondrák, W.
*1898 'Einige Bemerkungen anlässlich Meillet's "Recherches sur l'emploi du génitif-accusatif en vieux-slave"'. *ASP* 20.325–342.
Wackernagel, Jacob
*1926/1957 *Vorlesungen über Syntax.* Basel: Birkhauser.
Wählin, Hans
1926   *Wisby and the Ancient Civilization of Gotland.* Stockholm: Norstedt.
Watkins, Calvert
1965   'Lat. *nox* "by night": a Problem in Syntactic Reconstruction'. *Symbolae linguisticae in hon. G. Kuryłowicz.* (Polska AN, Prace komisji językoznawstwa, 5.) Pages 351–358.
Wertz, Christopher
1977   'The Number of Genders in Polish'. *Canadian Slavonic Papers* 19.50–63.
Worth, Dean S.
*1963/1977 'Linguistics and Historiography: a Problem of Dating in the Galician-

Volhynian Chronicle'. *Indiana Slavic Studies* 3.173–185. Reprinted in Worth 1977. Pages 221–235.

*1975 'O jazyke russkogo prava'. *VJa* 2.68–75. English translation 'On Russian Legal Language' in Worth 1977. Pages 257–265.

1977 *On the Structure and History of Russian. Selected Essays, with a Preface by Henrik Birnbaum.* Munich: Sagner (Slavistische Beiträge, 110).

(in press) 'Vernacular and Slavonic in Kievan Rus'.' *Slavonic Literary Languages. In Memory of Robert Auty and Anne Pennington.*

Xodova, Kapitolina I.

*1963 *Sistema padežej staroslavjanskogo jazyka.* Moscow: AN SSSR (In-t slavjano-vedenija).

Zaliznjak, A. A.

*1964 'K voprosu o grammatičeskix kategorijax roda i oduševlennosti v sovremennom russkom jazyĸe'. *VJa* 4.25–40.

*1967 *Russkoe imennoe slovoizmenenie.* Moscow: Nauka.

Other Books From
Slavica Publishers, Inc.

A. Nakhimovsky & R. Leed: *Advanced Russian.*

L. Newman, ed.: *The Comprehensive Russian Grammar of A. A. Barsov.*

F. J. Oinas, ed.: *Folklore, Nationalism & Politics.*

H. Oulanoff: *The Prose Fiction of Veniamin A. Kaverin.*

J. L. Perkowski: *Vampires of the Slavs.*

S. J. Rabinowitz: *Sologub's Literary Children: Keys to a Symbolist's Prose.*

L. A. Rice: *Hungarian Morphological Irregularities.*

D. F. Robinson: *Lithuanian Reverse Dictionary.*

R. A. & H. Rothstein: *Polish Scholarly Prose A Humanities and Social Sciences Reader.*

D. K. Rowney, ed.: *Russian and Slavic History.*

E. Scatton: *Bulgarian Phonology.*

W. R. Schmalstieg: *Introduction to Old Church Slavic.*

M. Shapiro: *Aspects of Russian Morphology, A Semiotic Investigation.*

O. E. Swan: *First Year Polish.*

C. E. Townsend: *Continuing With Russian, corrected reprint.*

C. E. Townsend: *Czech Through Russian.*

C. E. Townsend: *The Memoirs of Princess Natal'ja Borisovna Dolgorukaja.*

C. E. Townsend: *Russian Word-Formation, corrected reprint.*

D. C. Waugh: *The Great Turkes Defiance On the History of the Apocryphal Correspondence of the Ottoman Sultan in its Muscovite and Russian Variants.*

S. Wobst: *Russian Readings and Grammatical Terminology.*

J. B. Woodward: *The Symbolic Art of Gogol Essays on His Short Fiction.*

D. S. Worth: *Bibliography of Russian Word-Formation.*

M. T. Znayenko: *Gods of the Ancient Slavs Tatischev and the Beginnings of Slavic Mythology.*

American Contributions to the Eighth International Congress of Slavists Vol. 1: Linguistics & Poetics; Vol. 2: Literature.

P. M. Arant: *Russian for Reading.*

H. I. Aronson: *Georgian A Reading Grammar.*

Balkanistica: Occasional Papers in Southeast European Studies, Vol. III; Vol. IV; Vol. V; Vol. VI.

H. Birmbaum: *Common Slavic Progress and Problems in Its Reconstruction.*

H. Birnbaum: *Lord Novgorod the Great Essays in the History and Culture of a Medieval City-State, Part I The Historical Background.*

H. Birnbaum & T. Eekman, eds.: *Fiction and Drama in Eastern and Southeastern Europe.*

K. L. Black, ed.: *A Biobibliographical Handbook of Bulgarian Authors.*

M. Bogojavlensky: *Russian Review Grammar.*

R. C. Botoman: *Imi place limba Romana/ A Romanian Reader.*

E. B. Chances: *Conformity's Children An Approach to the Superfluous Man in Russian Literature.*

C. V. Chvany & R. D. Brecht, eds.: *Morphosyntax in Slavic.*

F. Columbus: *Introductory Workbook in Historical Phonology.*

R. G. A. de Bray: *Guide to the South Slavonic Languages.*

R. G. A. de Bray: *Guide to the West Slavonic Languages.*

R. G. A. de Bray: *Guide to the East Slavonic Languages.*

B. L. Derwing & T. M. S. Priestly: *Reading Rules for Russian.*

D. Disterheft: *The Syntactic Development of the Infinitive in Indo-European.*

J. S. Elliott: *Russian for Trade Negotiations with the USSR.*

J. M. Foley, ed.: *Oral Traditional Literature A Festschrift for Albert Bates Lord.*

Folia Slavica, a journal of Slavic, Balkan, and East European linguistics, 1977 ff.

R. Freeborn, ed.: *Russian and Slavic Literature.*

V. A. Friedman: *The Grammatical Categories of the Macedonian Indicative.*